The Open University

Social Sciences: a third level course
Regional analysis and development IV

Government Intervention

Unit 13 Methods of government intervention
Prepared for the course team by Gerald Manners

The Open University Press

Front cover: Publicity poster, Location of Offices Bureau

Back cover: Publicity advertisement by Tynemouth Corporation 1973

The Open University Press
Walton Hall, Milton Keynes
MK7 6AA

First published 1974 Reprinted 1975

Designed by the Media Development Group of the Open University.

Printed in Great Britain by
The Open University

ISBN 0 335 04897 8

This text forms part of an Open University course. The complete list of units in the course appears at the end of this text.

For general availability of supporting material referred to in this text, please write to the Director of Marketing, The Open University, P.O. Box 81, Walton Hall, Milton Keynes, MK7 6AT.

Further information on Open University courses may be obtained from the Admissions Office, The Open University, P.O. Box 48, Walton Hall, Milton Keynes, MK7 6AB.

1.2

Contents

Methods of government intervention

1 Introduction

Nearly all government policies, whether they are primarily economic or social in nature, tend to have a differential spatial effect. The priorities elected in a national fuel policy inevitably have a particular significance in the coalfield districts, just as a decision on the future of Concorde is bound to have a powerful bearing upon the short-term employment prospects of the Bristol region. Similarly, national policies designed to encourage a more frequent use of public transport are likely to have more far-reaching implications for large metropolitan areas than for the more remote parts of the country, whilst import levies on agricultural imports from non-EEC sources clearly have the greatest direct bearing upon the economic prospects of rural Britain. In this unit, however, interest will be centred upon those government decisions and actions that are deliberately designed to have a spatial impact. For, in a world that has come to accept an ever-increasing degree of public intervention in all aspects of life, one of the most fascinating trends is the growth of government intervention in the regional development process.

1.1 *Aim*

The aim of the unit, therefore, is to provide an introduction to the widening variety and growing complexity of the methods that can be used by governments in market and mixed economies to shape the geography of their economic and social life. A discussion of the measures used in the fully planned, or command, economies is reserved until later in the course (see Unit 16). The unit emphasizes the variety of scales at which government intervention can occur and, whilst there can be no complete analysis of the effectiveness of various measures in relation to their objectives, some indication is given of the major points of criticism that have been raised in response to experience to date.

1.2 *Objective*

The objective of the unit is to provide the student with a basic familiarity with the range of policy measures that have been adopted by the government of the United Kingdom in response to the country's geographical tendencies and problems. This is a key foundation upon which an understanding of the interaction of economic and social forces with political initiatives can be built. In addition, some indication is given of the use of similar policy measures in other countries, and of other forms of intervention that have not yet been tried in the British context.

2 The variety and scales of government intervention

Government measures specifically designed to induce local, regional or other spatial changes in economic and social life have multiplied in both their variety and their complexity in recent years. Compared with the tentative attempts made in Britain before World War II to influence the location of employment opportunities, to encourage population migration, to shape urban growth and to preserve open space for metropolitan populations, regional development policies today are infinitely more ambitious, more rigorous – and more expensive.

2.1 *The nature of the intervention*

The nature of this intervention in the evolution of a country's economic and social geography varies enormously with the precise motives and the related objectives of public policy. Consider, for example, a relatively isolated and old industrial community in northern England with severe structural unemployment that appears likely to persist. If the aims of a government are primarily social in nature, in the sense that it is thought desirable to reduce the misery and hardship there as quickly as possible, and to do it with relatively little regard to the longer-term costs of a policy decision, then the award of subsidies to prolong the life of the existing industries there might be judged to be the most relevant policy. If, on the other hand, economic considerations are judged to be of paramount importance, and the principal objective of public policy is to create a new and competitive economic base for the town, then actions that seek to steer into the locality a range of new employments in

5

some of the country's footloose growth industries would be most appropriately espoused.

Naturally, the motives and objectives of a government are constrained to some degree by its analysis of the problem that justifies its intervention. They are also shaped by the opportunities that are available for public initiatives. If the fundamental problem of the old industrial community postulated above is judged to stem from the locality's relative isolation from national markets and material or component suppliers, then a bold programme of road construction and perhaps of transport subsidies might well commend itself as an appropriate policy. If, in contrast, the failure of the town to attract an alternative economic base is seen to stem from a complex of environmental disadvantages – poor housing, old schools, limited amenities, a run-down shopping centre and an abundance of industrial and mining spoil-heaps – then the creation of a New-Town corporation and the allocation of funds for derelict land reclamation might be the preferred public response.

The adoption and the nature of such solutions are constrained, of course, by the opportunities for intervention that are available to a government in reality. A major programme of road construction, or the New-Town solution, might in some circumstances be ruled out by the limitations of the national budget and capital supply. The movement of new industries and jobs into the locality is obviously constrained by the total amount of industrial movement in any one year and the competing demands of other localities for those same footloose employments. The political climate of the day also bears heavily upon the adopted solution, since attitudes towards the permissible style of public intervention in regional development vary considerably through time, and from country to country. Much of what is politically acceptable in Britain in the 1970s would never have passed the test of acceptability in Britain thirty or forty years ago – and still remains politically unacceptable in Canada and the United States even today.

2.2 The scales of the intervention

Between macro-economic planning at the national scale, and the decisions taken within a locality concerning the evolution of land-uses, government can intervene in the development and resource-allocation process at a variety of scales. These scales range through a continuum from the largest geographical aggregations of space, short of the nation as a whole, down to small geographical disaggregations typified by a small city-region or the districts of the new county authorities in Britain. In Table 1, six Orders of spatial planning are hypothesized, and are illustrated with reference to the British case.

The First Order of spatial planning relates to the allocation of resources and divergences of public policies between the Assisted and Non-assisted Areas of the economy, a broad division of national economic space which need not necessarily generate geographically contiguous regions. As will be seen later, an increasing proportion of the country's resources in the years since World War II have been deliberately steered into the Assisted Areas by a multiplicity of government measures. These actions have stemmed from a variety of motives, some of which were economic (to employ unproductive labour resources and to counter inflationary tendencies in the more prosperous regions), others of which were social and political. A Second Order of spatial planning is concerned with the allocation of resources within each of these two broad divisions, between what might be called policy areas. Within the Assisted Areas, policy distinguishes between Northern Ireland, the Special Development Areas, the Development Areas and the Intermediate Areas, each of which is afforded a different level of public assistance to meet its problems and to adapt to changing economic circumstances. Similarly, with the Non-assisted Areas, there are zones of severe restraint and zones of only partial restraint (in terms of their development), together with a third, essentially neutral, type of area within which there are to be found neither restraints nor inducements to further development (on this particular scale). A Third Order of planning region, and one that is formally

Table 1 The scales of spatial planning

Scale continuum	Type of spatial planning	Principal concerns	Government departments	Type of plan
Large geographical aggregations ↑ ⋮ ⋮ ⋮ ⋮ ⋮ ⋮ ⋮ ⋮ ⋮ ↓ Small geographical disaggregations	(NATIONAL PLANS) *First Order* allocation between *broad divisions*: e.g. the Assisted and the Non-assisted Areas *Second Order* allocation between *policy areas*: e.g. Northern Ireland, Special Development Areas, Development Areas, Intermediate Areas in the Assisted Areas; severely restrained, partially restrained and neutral areas in the Non-assisted Areas *Third Order* allocation between *standard regions*: ten plus Northern Ireland in UK *Fourth Order* allocation between *sub-regions*: e.g. Highlands and Islands, Central Valley, Southern Uplands and Borders in Scotland; Greater London, the Green Belt, rest of Outer Metropolitan Area and Outer South East in South-East England *Fifth Order* allocation between *sub-divisions*: e.g. Glasgow, Falkirk, Stirling, Edinburgh in central valley of Scotland; North and South Humberside *Sixth Order* allocation between *districts*: e.g. within the Glasgow city-region: within the city-region of Kingston-upon-Hull (LOCAL PLANS)	Economic and political ↑ ⋮ ⋮ ⋮ ⋮ ⋮ ⋮ ⋮ ⋮ ↓ Environmental and social	Department of Industry Department of the Environment and Local Authorities	National planning Regional strategies Structure plans

recognized in the government's administrative and advisory machinery, is the standard economic region. In the case of the United Kingdom, there are ten of these regions, plus Northern Ireland. Government policy can, and clearly does, seek to influence the pattern of development between these regions, particularly through its control over major infrastructural investments such as roads and bridges, and through its willingness to approve their planning strategies and endorse such measures as the designation of New Towns.

Major sub-regions can be delineated, and public policies can be varied, within the standard regions, giving a Fourth Order of planning. In Scotland, for example, the Highlands and Islands, the Central Valley and the Southern Uplands and Borders are each subject to different government objectives and planning policies (Manners *et al* 1972 pp 387ff). Similarly, within South-East England public policy assumes a differential stance towards Greater London, the surrounding Green Belt and the rest of the Outer Metropolitan Area, and the Outer South East (Keeble 1972). Within the Yorkshire and Humberside planning region, there is a bold contrast between the characteristics, problems and growth possibilities of Humberside on the one hand, and of the older industrial zone of the West Riding of Yorkshire on the other; and between them, of course, lies a third sub-region of an essentially rural character (Warren 1972). Lower on the spatial scale than these sub-regions are the Fifth-Order sub-divisions. These are formally recognised for data-collection purposes by the government, and in the Scottish case they are called planning regions. Between these sub-divisions, public policies seek to shape the pattern of development and to allocate changes in population, employment, land-uses and the like in accordance with the statutory regional strategies and structure plans. The latter also provide guidelines for resource allocation at the lowest Order specified in Table 1, that is, between the districts that make up the sub-divisions.

These six Orders of spatial planning by no means afford a tidy, nested hierarchy of spatial disaggregation. At both the Fourth- and Fifth-Order scales, for example, it is sometimes necessary to analyse developments and plan across the boundaries of the Standard Economic Regions. The strategy for urban and economic development in North Buckinghamshire, which centres on the new city of Milton Keynes, is a typical case in point. Spatial planning is impoverished by rigid geographical sub-divisions and must always aspire to a highly flexible framework which can be adjusted to particular problems and developments. Nevertheless, the six Orders do serve to underline the variety of levels at which governments engage in spatial resource allocation, their activities interplaying with other forces in the space economy to espouse a variety of goals. As a generalization, we can say that the higher Orders of spatial planning tend to embrace economic and, to a lesser degree, political concerns and objectives; the lower Orders, on the other hand, are more concerned with environmental and social objectives. These tendencies are institutionalized, in the British case at least, in the government departments that are principally involved in spatial planning at different scales. As is indicated in Table 1, the first three Orders of planning are mainly handled by the Department of Industry (DOI), whereas the lower three Orders are more particularly the concern of the Department of the Environment (DOE) along with the local planning authorities over which it has considerable influence. Whilst recognizing, therefore, the continuum of scales at which spatial planning is pursued, we can usefully emphasize two fundamental sub-divisions – the inter-regional and the intra-regional. The detailed consideration that follows of the various methods that are used by governments in spatial planning is accordingly structured under these two headings.

3 Inter-regional intervention

One of the continuing debates in the field of regional development concerns the extent to which the problems of a region or locality stem from its spatial as opposed to its structural disadvantages (McCrone 1969 p 169). Consider the city-region of Plymouth, which has suffered throughout much of the post-World War II period from a relatively high level of unemployment: is this unemployment a function, more than anything else, of the relative remoteness of Plymouth from the country's major centres of industrial and office activity, i.e. a function of its space relationships? Or does the problem stem from the region's traditional industrial structure, with its high level of dependence upon the naval dockyard in which employment opportunities have steadily contracted? In the Plymouth case, as in many others, the answer lies in a subtle blend of the two factors. Nevertheless, the diagnosis of the nature of the problem inevitably influences the nature of the measures chosen by government to counteract it.

3.1 Spatial measures

To the extent that the spatial factor is judged to bear upon a particular regional problem or local difficulty, policy measures can be devised to reduce the burdens of a particular location and to adjust the meaning and the costs of space. By influencing the provision of transport facilities, and by manipulating the price of the service, governments have been able to change the economic prospects of particular areas, and to ensure a much more rapid rate of local and regional growth.

3.1.1 Infrastructural investments

Within the British context, there can be little doubt that the penetration of the motorway network into the Assisted Areas has had an enormously beneficial effect upon their medium-term economic prospects. The Severn Bridge and M4 into South Wales for example (Manners, 1966), and the M1, M18 and M62 into West Yorkshire have not only significantly lessened the cost of movement into and out of those regions, but have also had a profound psychological effect upon industrialists and developers by significantly reducing those regions' relative isolation. The major programme of road construction announced in June 1971, to expand the trunk-road and motorway programme throughout the whole country and so to provide 3,500 miles of strategic trunk routes, was in part justified by the contribution that it would make to the solution of the less prosperous regions' problems (House of Commons Expenditure Committee 1974 p 45). Similarly, in the United States it has been judged that one of the principal obstacles to the economic and social development of the depressed Appalachian region has been and remains its relative isolation from regions of rapid economic and urban growth. Despite its position between the prosperous megalopolis on the eastern seaboard and the generally healthy industrial economy of the Middle West, traffic has always tended to flow around Appalachia rather than through it. In consequence, of the more than $1,000 million of federal funds that were allocated to the region for assistance in the period 1965–71, some 75 per cent was provided for the construction of 2,300 miles of 'developmental highway' and 1,000 miles of local access roads. The rest of the money was shared between a variety of programmes concerned with health, land restoration, soil erosion control and hydrological surveys.

3.1.2 Transport pricing

The intervention of governments in the field of transport pricing, in order to assist particular localities or regions, can assume a variety of forms. A low level of transport charges may be granted to a region for goods shipped either into it or out of it, in order to compensate for its relative isolation and to assist its economic development. A case in point is provided by Eastern Canada, where in 1927 the Maritime Provinces were granted a 20 per cent reduction in their rail-freight rates to all other Canadian Provinces. The northern sections of Sweden similarly enjoy a central-government subsidy on all their transport costs. An alternative version of the same type of local or regional subsidy is the much more common national decision to maintain uniform rates over a whole transport system, irrespective of cost. In practice this means that, in effect, regions with a sparse population and limited traffic, or zones with difficult terrain and relatively high maintenance and operating costs, enjoy a cross-subsidy from the more densely-settled and economically more active parts of a country. An example is provided by the operations of British Rail in the Scottish Highlands, which are supported, not only by specific operating grants for specific lines paid for by the Ministry of Transport, but also by the freight-rate structure of the British system as a whole.

However, while there can be no doubt that the improvement of transport facilities and the reduction of transport costs to and from a problem region can significantly improve its prospects for development, there can be relatively few instances where additional initiatives are not required. Transport facilities and (relatively low) costs are undoubtedly an attractive feature for regional development, but they tend to be a permissive rather than an active component in the dynamics of economic growth. In other words, unless they permit the release of pent-up forces for change in a particular locality or region (and allow, for example, the economic exploitation of a natural resource for the first time), the transport components of a spatial-development policy must be supplemented by other public initiatives.

3.2 Structural measures

A second group of measures used in regional-development programmes are directed primarily towards the structural components of regional economic problems. In fact, they make up by far the greater part of the armoury of public weapons for tackling the geography of economic and social life. Measures in this category fall into three broad groups. First, there are those initiatives which are designed to assist the existing range of economic activities in a locality or region, to slow their decline, to stabilize their employment opportunities, and perhaps even to reverse their recent economic fortunes. A second group of measures is designed to provide an alternative range of economic activities by attracting new industries and offices into a problem area. A third, and less frequently publicized, group of measures place greatest emphasis upon population rather than on employment movement, and seek to encourage the movement of people away from a problem locality or region. Each of these three groups of measures will be discussed in turn.

3.2.1 Support for the existing economic base

In those instances where the difficulties of a regional economy stem from the stagnation or the decline of its staple trades, such as has been the case in the older industrial areas of Britain, an instinctive public response is to try to arrest that decline. To this end, markets can be artificially supported or increased by the purchasing policies of the government and nationalized industries, or sometimes by a protective international tariff. Alternatively, the operations of the industries can be subsidized directly or indirectly from the public purse, a solution which has found frequent expression in the case of nationalized concerns. Yet another approach is to provide government grants or loans, with the express intention that they should be used to restructure the industry so that it may be better able to withstand competition from other regions, foreign producers or substitute products – or from all three. The variety of government measures that are used to improve the position of a declining staple industry can be glimpsed through a brief review of some of the policies that have been adopted in Britain since World War II towards the coal, steel, cotton and shipbuilding industries, all of which are highly localized in the older industrial areas, have suffered from varying degrees of stagnation or decline, and, above all else, have offered fewer and fewer employment opportunities in places with limited alternative jobs.

The British *coal industry* has been the persistent beneficiary of public assistance throughout the post-war period, and more especially following its year of peak production in 1955. A whole range of *ad hoc* measures have been employed to protect the markets for coal. These include the heavy tax on its major competitor – fuel oil – and the government's occasional insistence that the Central Electricity Generating Board should burn substantial quantities of coal, in excess of its first preference and instead of further supplies of oil and natural gas that the Board would have preferred. In addition, following the publication of the 1967 White Paper on *Fuel Policy* (Minister of Power 1967), huge sums of public money were made available to permit the National Coal Board to plan a dignified retreat from many of the country's energy markets rather than suffer a traumatic defeat at the hands of lower-priced and more convenient fuels. By writing off the coal industry's debts, by slowing down the rate of mine closures, by offering financial assistance to those miners who were prepared to move from the high-cost to the low-cost coalfields, and by providing special assistance to attract new industries to locate in the coalfields (in newly-designated Special Development Areas), public policies prevented the financial collapse, alleviated much personal hardship in the industry, and thereby helped to preserve an important core of the British coal industry. Moreover, public capital – yielding very little financial return – was also used to reorganize the management, improve the skills, mechanize the operations and re-shape the geography of the production of the NCB, as it concentrated its remaining mining activities on its most efficient units, particularly those in the East Midlands and South Yorkshire. As it faced a changed set of opportunities in the middle 1970s, with the upward movement of energy prices, the British coal industry was of a size, and offered a range of employment opportunities in the less prosperous regions, that owed a great deal to persistent government support during the 1950s and 1960s.

Public policy has also shaped the size and the geography of the steel, shipbuilding and cotton industries, undoubtedly helping to retain in the less prosperous regions of the country employments which might otherwise have been lost or have been located elsewhere in the country. The classic case of public intervention in the affairs of the *steel industry* was in 1959, when a cabinet decision insisted that new strip-mill capacity should be shared between a publicly-owned company in South Wales (at

Llanwern) and a private company in Scotland (at Ravenscraig). Subsequently, when the greater part of the industry was brought under public ownership, a corporate plan was developed to indicate the most appropriate way in which the British Steel Corporation could meet the country's needs in the 1970s and 1980s. Economic, commercial, social and political criteria undoubtedly informed this huge and crucial exercise, and it is impossible to estimate what might have been the future shape of the industry without it. Two points are nevertheless clear. In the first place, access to public capital undoubtedly allowed much bolder planning, and, it was hoped, much better longer-term prospects for the industry, than would have been possible for a private industry earning a relatively low rate of return upon its capital investments. Secondly, dependence upon public capital and ultimate political sanctions undoubtedly constrained the locational options of the industry and meant that no serious attempt could be made to establish integrated steel-making in southern England – on lower Thameside or Southampton Water, for example – in a way that some observers thought worthy of consideration (Warren 1969a, 1969b).

In 1966 the Geddes Report on British *shipbuilding* stressed the need for a wholesale reorganization in response to sharpening foreign competition and the rising number of shipyard failures. It proposed the concentration of the industry into five regional groups, which would bring major economies of centralized design, purchasing and production control, and would permit a rationalization of the many separate workshops. The typical new production unit was to employ between 8,000 and 10,000 men and would handle 500,000 gross tons of ships each year. A year later the Shipbuilding Industry Board was set up, with access to over £200 million for use as a revolving credit to speed up the modernization of the yards, on the precondition that appropriate mergers within the industry and specific rationalization plans be carried out. Whilst it is impossible to be certain in these matters, there seems to be little doubt that, without the emergence of Scott-Lithgow and (after much trauma) Govan Shipbuilders on the Clyde, and the Swan Hunter and Tyne Shipbuilders, Austin and Pickersgill and the Doxford Group on the Tyne and Wear, the contraction of shipbuilding employment in Scotland and North-East England would have been much more acute, as a result of the wholesale collapse of the industry.

In a like manner, the government some years earlier, through the Cotton Industry Act of 1960, had made available some £30 million to rescue another staple industry that appeared powerless to save itself through its own initiatives. Characterized by a decade of mill closures and a huge inventory of old and half-used equipment, this Lancashire *cotton industry* was in urgent need of a major rationalization into fewer but larger production and marketing units, and of bold modernization. By offering compensation for the scrapping of machinery, the Act encouraged the abandonment of half of its spindles and 40 per cent of its looms, and, although re-equipment was slower than had been hoped, the proportion of automatic looms rose from 14 per cent in 1955 to 50 per cent in 1969. Unfortunately, the Act was less successful in encouraging rationalization in the industry, and it was only the force of industrial politics later in the decade – led by the major producers of artificial fibres, Courtaulds and Imperial Chemical Industries – that secured the financial and managerial revolution that was a precondition to further progress. Paradoxically, the fact that another arm of government regional policy had left most of Lancashire without Development-Area status (see below) meant that much of the recent investment in new plant and facilities has been outside Lancashire – and if there is a dominant growth region for the British textile industry today (since 1972 protected by a 15 per cent external tariff), it is Ulster (Rodgers 1972 pp 300 ff).

No aggregate figure can readily be produced to quantify the scale of deliberate public assistance over the years to the older staple industries that at one time flourished on the British coalfields, and that still provide a significant share of employment – especially male employment – in those regions. It is also impossible to measure or predict what would have been the size or the geography of these trades had there not been substantial public intervention in their affairs. Such uncertainties, however, must not detract from the fact that their employment levels would almost certainly have been much lower, nor underestimate the enormous cost and significance of the assistance provided by the government to these industries in its overall strategy of regional development.

3.2.2 Encouragement of new manufacturing employment

The second group of measures directed towards countering the structural weakness of an area's economy is concerned with encouraging the development of new manufacturing and office employments within it. The rationale of these measures is rooted in the belief that, for many lighter manufacturing and office activities, the private costs of production and operation, after an initial settling-in period, exhibit little variation between one part of a country and another. Partial location theory suggests, and various empirical studies, such as those conducted by Luttrell (1962), Toothill (Report of a Committee 1961) and Cameron and Clark (1966), have demonstrated, that a wide range of manufacturing enterprises are certainly in this category and can generically be termed 'footloose'. Moreover, since location questions are only a very small part of a total investment decision, and since they are frequently accorded a low level of investigation by many managements, the possibility exists that some manufacturers may be persuaded by public policy to consider them more seriously and perhaps even discover a location with a private cost advantage. In addition, of course, a significant social gain can be weighed in the equation, through a reduction of unemployment in the problem region and through a lessening of migration from it. The measures designed to steer new industries into a problem region, therefore, have to offset the disruptive costs of movement, and have to enhance the prospective financial gain of the entrepreneur in order to ensure his willingness to operate in a relatively alien environment. And once having attracted new industries into a problem locality, policy needs to ensure that expansion will actually occur there and not be drawn back to other regions of inherently more buoyant economic growth.

Measures have been designed to reduce the capital costs, the operating costs and the labour costs of industry moving to, or producing in, a problem region. Capital costs can be reduced by grants, loans and various types of tax concession such as an accelerated write-down of new investments against taxable profits. Operating costs can be reduced by the provision of low-cost or even free factory buildings, the externalities afforded by industrial estates, subsidized electricity and transport services. Labour costs, in particular, can be lowered through such schemes as a Regional Employment Premium, used in Britain for the first time from 1968, which provides firms with a *per caput* subvention on every person employed, and by funds to assist in the transfer of key workers to new manufacturing locations. Fashions change in regard both to the popularity of these various measures, and the particular blend which is judged to be the most appropriate for particular places at particular times.

In Britain, even over the last ten years, there have been substantial changes in the emphasis of the financial inducements offered to manufacturing industry to develop in problem areas. Between 1965 and 1967, the inducements to industrial development in the less prosperous regions were strongly biased towards offsetting the capital costs of manufacturing industry. The foundation-stone of government assistance was a 40-per-cent investment grant, which was 20 per cent higher than that available in southern England. The government was also prepared to give a building grant of up to 35 per cent of costs, to assist with the purchase of land. In addition, construction grants of 25 per cent were available, and these could be increased to 35 per cent if the firm concerned could provide evidence that it would employ a high percentage of male labour. Factories were also built ahead of demand – the so-called advance factories – and these could be either bought or rented at prices below those that would be commanded on the open market; in some localities these factories were available free of rent for up to five years. Following a move into a Development Area, loans were available to firms to ensure an adequate cash-flow during the initial settling-in period.

Criticism that this 'package' of government assistance was too heavily biased towards the subsidy of capital expenditure in the Development Areas, whereas the regions concerned were faced above all else with a problem of surplus labour, led to a novel measure introduced under the 1967 Finance Act. This gave manufacturers in the less prosperous regions a Regional Employment Premium, whereby their labour costs were subsidized to the weekly value of £1.50 per man employed, with rather smaller sums for women and adolescent employees. Not only did this arrangement give the manufacturer a 7-per-cent subsidy on his labour costs, but it had the attraction of being a continuing benefit rather than a once-and-for-all measure of support. Public money was also made available to provide housing in the less prosperous regions for those 'key' workers whose skills were not readily available in those regions and whom it was necessary to transfer with a migrant firm from other parts of the country.

Regional assistance to manufacturing industry was re-cast once again in 1970, following a desire to switch the emphasis of assistance away from direct grants to tax incentives, a step obviously favouring those firms which were commercially the most successful. By 1972, however, after further review of the system, the Industry Act – which sought to shape much of regional policy through to 1978 and full British membership of the European Economic Community – once again laid greatest stress upon the development grant, a much more predictable source of assistance to the industrialist and hence more persuasive to the potential mover. To the grant can be added various items of selective assistance when substantial increases in employment are proposed. Amongst these latter items are loans, interest-relief grants and removal grants. The changing magnitudes of the various investment incentives in the Development Areas of Britain, which followed from these shifts in policy, are recorded in Table 2. The varying size of the regional differential is all too apparent, as is the substantially higher level at which the arrangements settled down in 1972.

Table 2   Comparison of Investment incentives in the United Kingdom, 1969–1974 – the net present values of recoveries for grants and tax allowances, as a percentage of the cost of investments

	Pre-1970 %	1970–72 %	Since 1972 %
Development Areas			
Plant and machinery	49.8–52.4[1]	33.9	52.9
Industrial building	41.4	48.0	43.9
Mixed project[2]	48.1–50.2	36.7	51.1
Regional Differential[3]			
Plant and machinery	13.7–12.8	2.0	19.0
Industrial building	19.2	25.8	19.0
Mixed project	14.8–14.1	6.7	19.0

Notes:

1   The range relates to the lowest (15%) and the highest (25%) of the old writing-down allowances.

2   A mixed project assumes a ratio of plant to buildings of 4:1, the average for investment projects in manufacturing industry.

3   The recovery as a percentage of investment cost over and above what would be available in a non-assisted area.

NB   A discount rate of 10% has been assumed.

Source: *Hansard* Vol 835, No 99

Table 3 Summary of incentives for industry in the UK Areas for Expansion, 1974

Sector	Incentive	Special Development Areas	Development Areas	Intermediate Areas	Northern Ireland
Manufacturing:	Regional development grants:				Capital and industrial development grants
	New machinery, plant and mining works	22%	20%	Nil	
	Buildings and works (other than mining works)	22%	20%	20%	30% to 40%*
	Selective assistance Loans	On favourable terms for general capital purposes for projects which provide additional employment*; on non-preferential terms for other projects that maintain or safeguard employment if the finance required cannot reasonably be obtained from commercial sources.			On favourable terms for general purposes; loan guarantees may also be negotiated.*
	or interest relief grants*	As an alternative to loans on favourable terms, grants towards the interest costs of finance provided from non-public sources for projects which provide additional employment.			As in SDAs, DAs, IAs.
	Removal grants*	Grants of up to 80% of certain costs incurred in moving an undertaking into a Special Development or Intermediate Area.			Up to 100% of costs of transfer from place of origin.
	Government factories for rent or sale: rent-free period possible for certain new undertakings	Two-year rent-free period*			Rent-free period of 3 years and concessionary rent for further 2 years.*
	Employment grants	Nil			A substantial contribution paid during the initial build-up period to companies establishing attractive male-employing projects.
	Tax allowances: (a) Machinery and plant (b) Industrial buildings	100% first-year allowance on capital expenditure incurred on machinery and plant (other than private passenger cars). 44% of the construction costs can be written off in the first year and subsequently 4% per year. Note: These tax allowances apply to the country as a whole. Regional development grants in Great Britain for machinery and plant and buildings are not treated as reducing the capital expenditure in computing tax allowances; neither are the corresponding grants in Northern Ireland.			
	Finance from European Community funds	Loans may be available on favourable terms from the European Investment Bank (EIB) and the European Coal and Steel Community (ECSC).			
	Regional employment premium payable to manufacturers	£1.50 weekly for every male adult employee; lower rates for other employees.		Nil	As in SDAs and DAs.
	Training assistance	Special courses.			Free training courses at Government Training Centres; grants of £15 per male (£12 per female) per week for training on employers' premises.
	Help for transferred workers	Free fares, lodging allowances and help with removal expenses.			Full fares (inc. preliminary visit) and household removal costs (inc. legal fees) or lodging allowance plus substantial settling-in grants for key-workers from anywhere outside Northern Ireland.
	Contracts preference schemes	Benefits from contracts placed by government departments and nationalised industries		Nil	As in SDAs and DAs.
Service:	Service industry removal assistance	For offices, research and development units, and other service industry undertakings moving into the assisted areas, a fixed grant of £800 for each employee moving with his work, up to a 50% limit, and a grant to cover the cost of approved rent of premises in the new location for up to 5 years in a Special Development Area and up to 3 years in an Intermediate Area. (Projects helped under this scheme are not eligible for help under the key workers scheme.)			Flexible range of assistance under the Industries Development Acts (Northern Ireland) 1966 and 1971.

Note:
Incentives marked * are subject to the provision of sufficient additional employment to justify the assistance sought.

Source: Department of Trade and Industry (1974)

The full range of government incentives for manufacturing industries in what are now called the 'Areas for Expansion' are recorded in Table 3. It should be noted that, although the Regional Employment Premium is scheduled to be phased out over a period from September 1974, influential voices on both sides of industry have been appealing for its retention as a permanent feature of regional-development policies. Present incentives also include special courses and grants for the training of local labour and a preferential position for firms in the Assisted Areas at the negotiation of government contracts. Loans may also be available on favourable terms from the European Investment Bank and the European Coal and Steel Community.

Paralleling these measures designed specifically to induce particular firms to move into, or to expand in, the less prosperous regions, public policy has also sought to improve the overall attactiveness of these areas to manufacturing enterprise. Externalities are offered through the grouping of many firms on industrial estates. The general quality of labour supply is improved through Government Training Centres, highly localized in the less prosperous regions and now offering 18,000 places each year. Industrial Expansion Teams, under the (DOI) Industrial Development Executive, give advice about homes, schools and other facilities in particular areas, as well as affording specialist advice to industry. Major efforts have been made to improve the quality of the transport infrastructure, by constructing new roads, encouraging the development of liner-train services and supporting the development of regional air services. Significant progress has been made to improve the general quality of the environment, through the improvement of derelict mining areas and the removal of derelict industrial buildings and plant. The quality of life generally in the less prosperous parts of the country has been significantly improved through the support given to a widening range of regional artistic and cultural activities by such bodies as the Arts Council. All these advances have been stressed in a sustained advertisement programme which has sought to emphasize the many assets of the Areas for Expansion for industrial development.

3.2.3 Encouragement of new service employment

For many years the main emphasis of British policy towards inter-regional disparities was upon the encouragement of indigenous or mobile manufacturing industry in the less prosperous regions. With time, however, it came to be recognized that, not only could service employments also assist regional development, but they were becoming increasingly important as the national rate of employment-growth in manufacturing activities slowed down. The first candidates for government attention were naturally public employments themselves, and in the early 1960s plans were set afoot to move substantial blocks of work away from central London. In the Fleming Report of 1962 it was recommended that 14,000 posts should be moved from central London, of which 5,500 should be to the outskirts, on the grounds that their effectiveness would not be impaired by their separation from the central Departments in Whitehall. An even more determined search for additional candidates for decentralization was conducted in the early 1970s with the Hardman enquiry (Hardman 1972), and the proposal was made to relocate some 31,000 jobs, of which 12,100 would be to locations in South-East England. These intiatives by the government towards its own activities, were complemented only as recently as 1973 by the offer of inducements to the private office sector to expand in the less prosperous regions. In those instances where office projects have a genuine choice of location either inside or outside an Assisted Area, and where they will provide at least 10 new jobs in an Assisted Area, removal grants are now available to the value of £800 per employee moved with his work, and a selective grant is available to cover the cost of approved rent for a period of up to 5 years. In addition, a grant may be given to cover up to 80 per cent of the costs of moving office plant and machinery, stocks and materials, as well as the employer's net statutory redundancy payments at his old location.

3.2.4 Development restraints – floorspace controls

One of the features of British measures designed to attract new activities into the less prosperous regions has been to set alongside these many inducements to growth in the areas themselves a number of restraints upon the expansion of manufacturing and office activities in the more prosperous parts of the country. To the pull of inducements has been added the push of floorspace controls, and in this regard British practice is quite unique in Western Europe. Manufacturing industry was the first element in employment location to be subject to such controls. Independently of any local planning permission (see section 4.1), from 1947 any manufacturer wishing to construct an industrial building of more than 465 square metres (5,000 sq ft) or wishing to expand his existing premises by more than 10 per cent has had to obtain an industrial development certificate from the Department of Trade (originally the Board of Trade). There has been no blanket refusal of permissions in the South East and the West Midlands, each application being viewed on its merits, and there have been variations through time in the size of plant for which permission was required. From 1965 similar controls have been applied to office buildings, for which an office development permit has had to be obtained from the Department of the Environment (or its predecessors) before any new office building or conversion involving more than 353 square metres (3,000 sq ft) could proceed. Once again, through time there have been variations in the exact specifications and geography of these controls (Manners 1972a pp 19 ff).

No one would deny that these floorspace controls have been singularly persuasive in encouraging industrial and (to a lesser extent) office movement in Britain. However, many observers view them with some disquiet, because of the distortions which they tend to generate in the firm and economy alike. For example, many firms, in order to avoid the controls, have kept their new buildings just below the threshold-size requiring permission, if they have been on a new site; or they have stayed in old and inadequate premises. This has not necessarily been good for their productivity. Moreover, to the extent that the controls added a further round of delays and bureaucratic procedures to the process of national development, and to the extent that administrative judgements in considering each case on its merits could sometimes prove to be naive, doubts have arisen concerning the wider costs of the control mechanism. Certainly, in the case of offices there is little doubt that within a few years of its introduction the floorspace-control system had become a major factor in creating a growing scarcity of office space in the South East, which was reflected in substantial rises in the cost of accommodation there (Manners 1972b). Above all, however, the view has increasingly been taken that even flexible controls relating to industrial or office *floorspace* are not necessarily the most appropriate to influence the size and geography of manufacturing and office employment. Over the years, therefore, greater emphasis came to be placed upon the use of incentives in the regions of reception, rather than on controls in the regions of more natural development. The controls have been retained nevertheless, in order to encourage employers to consider alternative locations and out of a fear that the incentives elsewhere might of themselves be insufficient to bring about sufficient industrial movement in the desired direction.

3.2.5 *Persuasion*   Inducements to industrial movement have been supported by two further public initiatives. First has been public persuasion. By means of press advertising in particular, but also through films, television and displays, the government has sought to demonstrate to the entrepreneur some of the more positive advantages of the less prosperous parts of the country. Their labour supplies, their amenities, the easy access which they afford to outstanding natural environments and their lower costs of housing have all been stressed. From the outset the Location of Offices Bureau (see section 4.7), which has the distinctly narrow remit to encourage offices to leave central London and which has only more recently become committed to inter-regional as opposed to intra-regional objectives, has spent about half of its budget on advertising.

To the persuasion of the central-government departments in these matters there have been added the campaigns of regional bodies, local authorities and development corporations in the less prosperous regions themselves, seeking to draw attention to the particular attractions of their localities. Hence the familiarity of such names as the North East Development Council, the Mid-Wales Industrial Development Association, the Scottish New Towns and the like. (See also the advertisements reproduced on page 18.)

A final weapon in a government's armoury is direct and private persuasion. With immediate access to senior management in both the public and private sectors of the economy, government can intervene directly on behalf of its locational policies to considerable effect. A classic instance in Britain occurred in the period 1958–1960, when the motor-car industry was on the verge of major expansion. Its first preference, naturally, was to extend its facilities adjacent or near to its existing assembly lines in the West Midlands and Greater London. Denied this preference by the industrial development certificate controls, an extended round of negotiations at the highest levels of government produced a compromise solution: some expansion of production facilities was allowed in the more prosperous regions in return for major investments in the motor industry in several of the country's Development Areas. The major beneficiary of this bargain was Merseyside, which obtained the plants of Ford, Vauxhall and Standard-Triumph – investments that by 1970 had cost some £160 million and that directly employed over 30,000 workers. Scotland and Wales benefited from these negotiations also, with Chrysler and the British Motor Corporation opening plants at Linwood and Bathgate in Scotland, and the British Motor Corporation, Ford and Rover investing heavily in South Wales.

Again, in 1966–67, when the international aluminium industry expressed a serious interest in British locations for the first time (an earlier, but much smaller, investment remains at Fort William in Scotland), political pressures strongly influenced the outcome – both in the scale of investment and in its location. Following upon a series of complicated negotiations with the electricity-generating authorities and the National Coal Board, the industry elected to develop three sites (rather than two, which was its original preference) at Invergordon in Scotland, Lynemouth in Northumberland and on Anglesey in North Wales. Whether the direct and indirect public costs of these decisions can ever be matched by the local employment benefits generated by the smelter, however, remains very much an open question (Manners 1968).

In those countries where state-owned enterprise extends well beyond what might be regarded as the traditional sphere of public ownership in the mixed economies, public policies are provided with a further set of opportunities for the direct persuasion of management. In the Italian case, in fact, this has been compounded into a more general requirement that all state industries should invest at least 60 per cent of their incremental capacity in the problem regions of the south.

3.2.6   *Migration policy*   A third broad set of responses to the problems posed by the structural characteristics of a locality or region involves the acceptance of fewer employment-opportunities there, and it seeks to facilitate the movement of population away to other regions in the country. In a sense this is simply encouraging what is in any case the instinctive reaction of many of the people in the problem regions. At the same time, it is also a recognition that there exists within an unemployed population an element that will move only if knowledge of employment-opportunities elsewhere is made more widely available, and if some financial assistance is provided to reduce the costs of migration. A good deal of voluntary labour migration occurs with the assistance of private employers, who seek to attract workers from the problem localities through normal press advertising. Some large employers often assist the movement of their workers from localities of redundancy to other areas where jobs are available; the National Coal Board, for example, has for many years sought to encourage the transfer of miners from the high-cost mining areas of Scotland, North-East England and South Wales to the newer and more productive mining regions of the East Midlands.

18

In most countries, migration policies are both tentative and weakly developed. Britain is no exception. For example, compared with the £2,000 million that the government claimed to have injected into the economy over the two-year period 1970–72 for the express purpose of job creation, less than £3 million was spent on encouraging labour mobility. In 1972 only 7,500 people made use of the government's schemes, though that same year also saw the decision to increase expenditure annually to £5 million. In Britain grants are available to workers in industrial-training schemes that involve a change of home; and grants are also available to workers in development areas who are prepared to move either within their regions, or beyond their regions, in order to secure employment. The grant for the latter is £400. It is to be compared with a cost of establishing a new job in a problem area, for which estimates range from £2,000 to £6,000. Small but growing, this migration assistance is a natural – if underdeveloped – counterpart to the more publicized policies of getting the work to the workers. In an ever more fluid geography of employment, its importance seems more likely to grow than to diminish (Salt 1973).

3.3 *The geography of assistance*

Measures designed to assist regions or localities in distress need to be made applicable to carefully designated geographical areas. Historically, the criterion has invariably tended to be some level of unemployment within a local authority or other administrative area. Through time, however, the inadequacy of such a crude index has been exposed; it neglects such indices of need as a high level of out-migration, a low activity rate, relatively low levels of income and, in agricultural areas especially, evidence of high levels of underemployment (Secretary of State for Economic Affairs 1969). The definition of problem areas eligible for public assistance, therefore, has come to be much more broadly based in recent years. The draft proposals of the criteria that will guide the geography of aid from the regional fund of the European Economic Community are summarized in Table 4; it is the qualifying areas that will be able to receive loans from the European Investment Bank, assistance from the Social Fund for the resettlement and retraining of workers, and the attention of the proposed regional-development company that will act as a minority shareholder on a temporary basis in companies set up in development areas.

Table 4   Draft criteria for areas within the European Economic Community that will be eligible for regional aid

Two general criteria applicable in all circumstances:
1 The locality must be included within a national system of regional aids
2 The locality must have a gross domestic product per head below the community average

Additional criteria, one of which must be applicable:
1 The locality must have a preponderance of agricultural activities, defined as having more people working in farming and fewer people in industry than the Community average
2 The locality must be undergoing industrial change, with at least 5,000 people making up at least 20 per cent of the workforce employed in textiles and coalmining; such areas must also either suffer from unemployment above the Community average or have a high level of emigration
3 The locality must be suffering structural unemployment. The criteria here are (a) a GDP per head of less than half the community average, (b) net emigration of over 1 per cent per year over at least 4 years, or (c) a rate of unemployment of at least 3.5 per cent and at least 1.2 times the national average

All the criteria can be applied only to localities with at least 100,000 people and 500 square kilometres (193 sq. mls.).

Source: *The Economist* October 13 1973 p 70

A locality or region with a problem of unemployment or out-migration is not necessarily entitled to assistance in order to attract alternative industries and jobs. The locational requirements of industry change through time, as do the locational preferences of society, and it can sometimes be the case that a problem locality cannot or should not be subject to policies seeking to provide a new economic base. Yet another facet of public measures designed to assist problem regions, therefore, is the need to designate and delimit those localities that are suitable for redevelopment. In the United States, for example, under the 1965 Public Works and Economic Development Act, assistance is available to what are known as Economic Development Districts; these have to be a group of adjacent counties that not only meet certain criteria relating to high levels of unemployment and average incomes, but also include one urban centre that has the potential to develop. British policy has also sought to adopt policies that specially encourage redevelopment in some of the more attractive parts of the less prosperous regions. It has also been somewhat contradictory, however, and only on a few occasions has it been judged politically expedient to develop plans based explicitly on the notion of a growth centre or growth pole.

The first localities to be designated for public assistance in Britain were the so-called Special Areas of the 1930s. The principal criterion used in their delimitation was the level of local unemployment. In consequence, because the largest urban centres in South Wales, North-East England and Central Scotland were not so badly hit by the decline of the staple trades as their hinterlands, these regional capitals were excluded from government assistance. With the Distribution of Industry Act of 1945, however, Development Areas were defined on a regional basis; as a result Cardiff, Newcastle and Glasgow, cities upon whose economic performance the future of their surrounding regions heavily depended, were included in the designated areas. Neglecting the policy variations of the period from 1958–62 (Manners 1972a p 55), this trend of policy to designate larger regions within which assistance could be made available was pushed further forward throughout the 1960s, until today the Assisted Areas embrace the whole of Northern Ireland, Scotland and Wales, all of Yorkshire and Humberside, the North-West and the Northern planning regions, and parts of the South West and the East Midlands (Figure 1). The year 1963, and the publication of the two White Papers on North-East England and Central Scotland (Secretary of State for Industry, Trade and Regional Development 1963; Secretary of State for Scotland 1963), saw a further shift in emphasis away from the initial instinct to channel assistance to the worst-hit localities within a region. In those White Papers the government for the first time elected to give most support to those localities within the Development Areas that appeared to be the most attractive from the point of view of development. Thus, a 'growth zone' was defined in North-East England, and 'growth centres' were designated in Central Scotland, and a commitment was made to channel the greater part of infrastructural investments into those areas in the hope that it would there attract most new employments and create the best conditions for longer-term, self-sustaining growth. Although the subsequent regional plans and strategies of the less prosperous regions have been somewhat less explicit in their geographical ambitions, the growth-area approach remains a feature – even if, for local political reasons, a somewhat muted feature – of regional planning in the Assisted Areas today.

The need to determine a preferred geography of redevelopment within a problem region has its counterpart at the inter-regional scale. Regional problems have differing degrees of severity; and their solutions imply differing degrees of assistance. In several countries, therefore, it has been found desirable to provide regional assistance at different levels, according to a set of variable criteria. The current geography of the British case is illustrated in Figure 1. It can be seen that the Assisted Areas are sub-divided into four categories – Northern Ireland, the Special Development Areas, the Development Areas and the Intermediate Areas. The different levels of assistance to each of these four categories is shown in Table 3 (p 14).

Figure 1   The Areas for Expansion in the United Kingdom, 1974

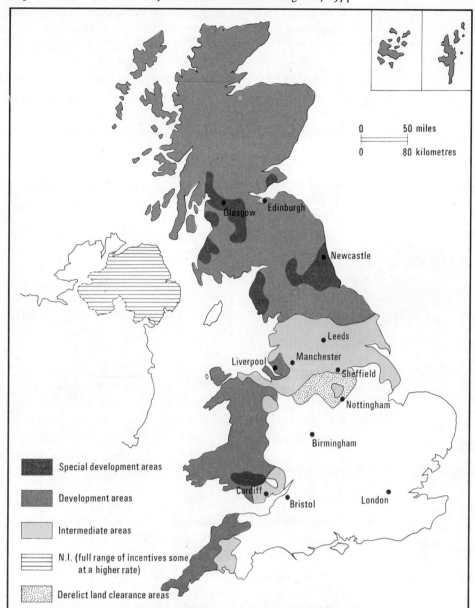

Similarly, for development-aid purposes France has been divided into five, only partly contiguous, zones. These are illustrated in Figure 2, with zone A being eligible for the highest levels of assistance in both the manufacturing and service sectors. It will be noted that an extensive area around Paris, plus a much smaller area around Lyons, make up what is in fact a sixth zone, in which there exist significant constraints upon development. Lyons itself, on the other hand, is one of a designated set of major provincial centres in which tertiary developments are either permitted or encouraged.

3.4   *The effectiveness of the measures*

The effectiveness – and more particularly the cost-effectiveness – of the various measures taken by government to improve the inter-regional balance of employment-opportunities and economic growth remains a subject for considerable debate. Examining British experience recently, the House of Commons Expenditure Committee (1973 p 72) were not convinced that the continuing search for a viable regional policy has been backed by a critical economic apparatus capable of analysing results and proposing alternative courses. They concluded:

Much has been spent and much may well have been wasted. Regional policy has been empiricism run mad, a game of hit-and-miss, played with more enthusiasm than success. We do not doubt the good intentions, the devotion even, of many of those who have struggled over the years to relieve the human consequences of regional disparities. We regret that their efforts have not been better sustained by the proper evaluation of the costs and benefits of policies pursued.

Figure 2   Zones for regional development aid in France, 1974. Source: DATAR (Délégation à l'Aménagement du Territoire et à l'Action Régionale)

The legend indicates regionalization of financial assistance, with aid increasing between zones E to A. Squares indicate provincial urban centres designated for substantial expansion

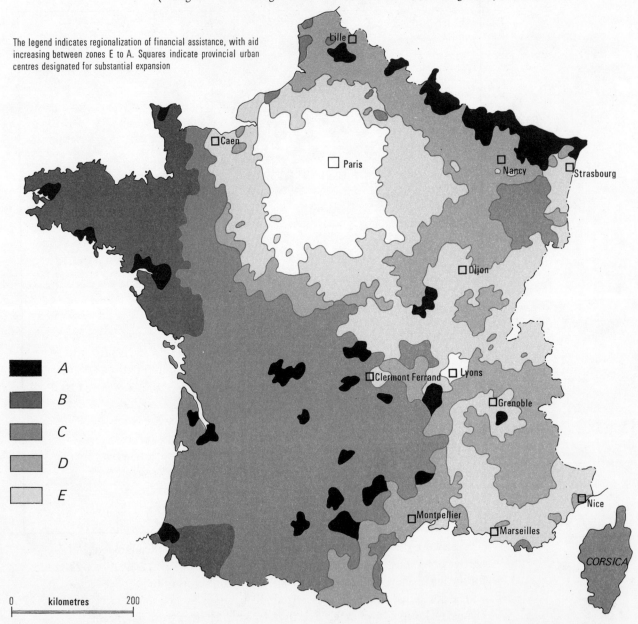

3.4.1   The costs of inter-regional programmes

The costs of regional programmes can only be partly measured, as was noted earlier. Direct Exchequer expenditure on regional-development loans, grants, tax allowances, the regional employment premium and the like, are of course known. The White Paper *Public Expenditure to 1976–77* contains the figures shown in Table 5 (1972 survey prices). To these figures has to be added the regional component of outstanding investment grants, and the regional differential in depreciation allowances relevant to the period October 1970–March 1972; both of these will substantially increase the effective 1972–73 costs.

In contrast to this fairly firm data, several kinds of indirect expenditure by the government in the Assisted Areas for regional-development purposes cannot be easily quantified. Differential expenditure on infrastructure; assistance to the coal, steel, cotton and shipbuilding industries; and many other sectoral policies which have a significant regional impact in the less prosperous parts of the country – all are omitted from the figures. However, the expenditure data that are available are all 'net

Table 5 Proposed direct Exchequer expenditure on regional development assistance in the United Kingdom, 1972–73 to 1976–77

(£m.)

	1972–73	1973–74	1974–75	1975–76	1976–77
Regional development grants	28	225	230	255	275
Expenditure under Local Employment Acts (LEA)	63.4	54.6	22.6	9	5
Selective regional assistance	10	35	45	60	60
REP	100.9	95.7	64.9	2	—
Totals	202.3	410.3	362.5	326	340

Source: House of Commons Expenditure Committee (1974)

of clawback', that is, they do not take into account the additional tax receipts and national-insurance contributions that will arise from the increased output and employment generated by regional policies; nor do they recognize the effects of a reduction in unemployment benefits. Moore and Rhodes (1973) have estimated that the size of the 'clawback' was as much as £166 million per year during the 1960s.

There are, of course, other costs of regional policy that are not carried by government. No monetary calculation can possibly reflect the costs of frustrated developments in the more prosperous parts of the country. No measures are available of the productivity of firms steered into the less prosperous regions as compared with what their productivity might have been in South-East England or the West Midlands. Whilst some firms have undoubtedly gained financially from a move to the Development Areas, others have had to pay a continuing cost. In their evidence to the Expenditure Committee (House of Commons p 17) all four major motor-car manufacturers claimed that there was a continuing net cost to be carried by their operations in the Development Areas; for the British Leyland group alone it was estimated that the current net cost of their Development-Area operations was about £4.7 million per year, after receipt of the Regional Employment Premium.

3.4.2   *The benefits*   On the benefit side of the equation, uncertainties are equally abundant. Estimates of job creation by government initiatives in the less prosperous regions are subject to wide margins of error. Besides the difficulty of putting a figure to the number of jobs retained in the older staple trades there, much uncertainty surrounds the magnitude of the secondary employment which is generated, both in the form of linked development (such as the expansion of existing firms in the Merseyside region to serve the incoming motor industry) and through the multiplier effects on the tertiary sector (the need for more teachers, doctors, waiters and the like than would have been the case without the government-induced basic employments). To the extent that development is diverted from regions where there is intense pressure on labour and land resources, and from whence national inflationary pressures might in some measure originate, there are yet further benefits to be recorded – but they too remain unquantified.

So many of the changes in a country's economic geography stem from factors other than regional policy – from movements in transport charges, from changing attitudes towards distance and geographical space, from new evaluations of the quality of provincial life, and the like – that a final balance-sheet of government attempts to stimulate regional development in the less prosperous parts of a country will never be drawn up. Notwithstanding the difficulties facing policy evaluation, it is nevertheless clear that many more attempts will have to be made to establish with greater certainty the effectiveness of alternative public policies in a country's inter-regional development strategy. Prospectively, the scarce financial resources of the public purse allocated to regional programmes must be better employed, and policies would clearly benefit from a greater certainty about their full effects.

4 Intra-regional intervention

Major infrastructural investments and social overhead capital are inevitably funded out of the public purse. In consequence, it is in the community's interest to make sure that those facilities are neither unnecessarily under-utilized nor heavily overloaded. Apart from this consideration, and the occasional interest shown by planners in the economics of city size or in spatial productivity variations (Greater London Council 1969), government intervention in the processes of regional development at the intra-regional scale rarely occurs for economic reasons. More usually it is concerned with environmental, social and aesthetic issues. The three principal devices used by governments at the intra-regional scale are the allocation of land uses and development control, positive initiatives in shaping the pattern of urban growth, and decisions concerning transport and other infrastructural investments. These can be supplemented by measures designed to alter the locational pattern of public employments, by the judicious use of floorspace controls on manufacturing and office developments and, once again, by the gentle art of persuasion.

4.1 The planning framework

In all countries the nature of government intervention is severely constrained by the institutional framework within which physical and regional planning is conducted. In Britain, for example, since the Town and Country Planning Act of 1968 spatial planning has been conducted within a three-tier system. At the highest and most generalized level, regional strategies are produced. These relate to the new standard regions and are prepared by a team of officials from both the Department of the Environment and the local authorities concerned; it is sponsored by the Regional Economic Planning Council and the standing conference of local planning authorities in the region concerned. Beneath the regional strategy, and consistent with it, come the structure plans. These are prepared by the local planning authorities (the metropolitan and the non-metropolitan counties) and relate to the county areas. They are essentially a statement of general geographical intent, but are not an accurate design upon the map. Below these are the grass-root plans, the detailed land-use allocations which do involve drawing firm lines on Ordnance Survey maps, and which show how urban and rural land-uses will be permitted to change in the foreseeable future. To this three-tier arrangement there has been added a 'mezzanine floor'; this is the use, discussed earlier, of industrial development certificates and office development permits by the Departments of central government to influence developments within regions as well as between them. The mezzanine floor thus provides mechanisms that can assist in the realization of both the regional strategies and the sub-regional structure plans. It is within this legal and institutional framework, then, that many of the means of government intervention at the intra-regional scale are applied in Britain. In other countries, such as the United States for example, the framework is more varied (from State to State), on the whole simpler (with single-tier zoning authorities allocating local land-uses), and generally rather restrictive as regards the range of initiatives that government can take. For this reason especially, the present section concentrates heavily upon British example and experience.

4.2 Land-use and development controls – green belts

One of the boldest and better-known devices for influencing the pattern of intra-regional development through land-use and development controls is the designation of a green belt. The idea of a green belt was initially associated with the growth of London, since it was with the checking of the ever-spreading character of the metropolis that the early advocates of the measure – men such as Ebenezer Howard and George Pepler (Thomas 1970) – were largely concerned. Subsequently, however, the idea commended itself to local authorities in many parts of the country, and it has come to exert a major influence upon the density and the geography of urban development throughout Britain. By rigorously denying permission for 'non-conforming' uses to locate or be extended within a green belt, local planning authorities have been able to retain the essentially rural character of substantial tracts of country that would otherwise have fallen to suburban development, and achieve an outward preservation of much of the existing quality of the landscape.

The notions that lie behind the designation of a green belt can be quite varied. When Ebenezer Howard and his associates were writing at the turn of the present century, they intended in part that the delimitation of a green belt would prevent the inordinate growth of a city beyond the point where its services became uneconomically overloaded; they also saw a rural zone surrounding a town as a means of preserving agricultural land and so a means of securing that urban area's food supply; and a third purpose of a green belt, according to Howard and his associates, was to preserve the countryside near to a city for recreational purposes. In contrast, other writers at the turn of the century were anxious to introduce an open-space rural ring into the development of a city, on the assumption that, beyond this zone of relative tranquillity, urban development would be allowed to continue unchecked. Yet another concept of the green belt, and one that has in fact been adopted around Edinburgh, envisages a zone of rural land which is protected against urban development; but over time this zone is adjusted outwards to allow for further urban growth. The chief purpose of this 'crawling' green belt is to prevent ribbon development and scattered growth on the urban fringe.

When a former Minister of Housing and Local Government (a department now absorbed into the DOE) published an official circular on green belts in 1955, attention was drawn once again to their value for physically restraining continued urban and suburban sprawl. In addition, however, it was suggested that green belts might usefully be designated in order to stop the merging of nearby towns and cities, and also to preserve the special character of historic and unique urban environments, places such as Cambridge, Oxford and York.

4.2.1 *Some criticisms*   The value and success of green-belt policies has been widely acclaimed. Nevertheless, criticisms of both a specific and a general nature have been levelled at them. Specific criticisms have related to the functioning of green belts in particular places. When the population and housing pressures of the Greater London area began to approach, and in some senses exceed, the land available for those uses, by the middle 1960s, some observers argued for a more flexible attitude towards the green belt's boundaries on the urban fringe. By yielding 1 per cent of the green belt, homes could be provided for 150,000 people; the attractions of such a trade-off were obviously substantial to those whose primary concern was for more housing. Again, the green-belt controls imposed over the little-used estuarine marshes between Cardiff and Newport in South Wales have been criticized for their sterilization of what might otherwise have been extremely valuable industrial land in a sub-region that badly needed further manufacturing investment.

More general criticisms of green belts relate to the somewhat confused purposes for which they have at times been designated. In so far as the economics and aesthetics of urban size are open to debate, it is not surprising that green belts have been imposed around towns and cities of varying sizes – from London at one extreme to quite small communities such as Bath at the other. They have implied, and the planning authorities sometimes have asserted, that the existing size of the contained urban area was in some sense large enough – even ideal – and that any momentum for further growth should be deflected to other places. Naturally, local and regional interests can diverge on these matters, and the result has been that the creation and retention of a green belt has become in many places the focus of a vigorous and acrimonious debate. In fact, green-belt policies have in many instances proved to be nothing more than an institutionalization of one of the persistent themes of land-use debate and planning in the last quarter-century, that is, the conflict between urban and rural interests. Thus, in the West Midlands the local authorities surrounding the conurbation have used the mechanism of the green belt, as a means of containing urban expansion, for local political as much as for regional-planning reasons.

Whilst it is easy to specify in general terms that development applications within a green belt should be allowed only if they are concerned with (what have come to be called) 'conforming' uses – activities that will allow the functional and landscape qualities of the belt to be preserved – in practice such a formula is open to a variety of interpretations. To start with, when they are first designated, green belts already perform a wide variety of functions and are characterized by a complex geography of land uses. Agricultural pursuits exist alongside mineral workings, transport facilities (including airfields), recreational facilities such as golf courses, and a variety of institutional, residential and commercial activities. Schools, hospitals, farms, cemeteries, country retreats, sewage works, railway lines, sand and gravel pits, water-pumping stations, army camps, commuters' homes, agricultural labourers' cottages – and many other uses – all abound in designated green belts. With the purpose of the belts not always clearly specified, it is far from easy for a local planning

Figure 3   The green belts of South-East England, 1974   Source: Department of the Environment (1973)

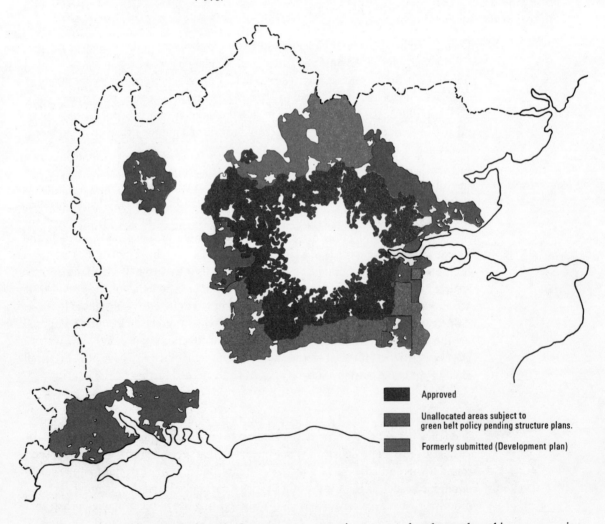

Approved

Unallocated areas subject to
green belt policy pending structure plans.

Formerly submitted (Development plan)

officer to decide whether or not an extension to a sand and gravel working, a new wing on a mental hospital, three more farm workers' cottages (which might in time become middle-class weekend retreats), or an extension to an airfield are in fact conforming uses and should be allowed. Given the pressures for change in the land uses around a metropolitan area such as Greater London, the green belt of which is illustrated in Figure 3, few would deny that the local planning authorities have performed the remarkably difficult task of holding the green belt with outstanding skill and overall success. It is inevitable, however, that many of their individual decisions should have been the object of criticism and that evidence of inconsistency in handling planning applications is not difficult to find.

No aspect of green-belt policy has been subject to more debate than its recreational role. Whilst the land in a green belt is in part reserved for this purpose, its ownership generally remains in private hands. In consequence there are frequently conflicts between the public and the private interest which in the last resort can be resolved only through the public ownership of at least some green-belt land. As early as the 1930s, in fact, the London County Council began to purchase land beyond its own territory in order to provide for the recreational needs of the metropolis. This early initiative has not been followed through in the years since World War II, either through further acquisitions or through more deliberate attempts to make the land already in public ownership serve more fully in a recreational role. However, the view has become increasingly widespread recently that local authorities must in future place more emphasis upon the positive functions of the green belts, investing money to develop recreational opportunities in particular, and also removing some of the eyesores such as derelict land that presently characterize parts of many green belts around the country.

4.2.2 *Other land-use controls*

Over the years several other land-use designations have been espoused in an attempt to preserve the character of particular localities and to steer housing and urban development into other places. Areas of Outstanding Natural Beauty have been designated, for example; within these the quality of the natural (or tamed natural) environment can be more rigorously defended against development pressures. Lengthy tracts of the coastline are also now subject to specific planning controls that seek to preserve, and in places repair, this particular feature of the country's scenic heritage. Local authorities are now in a position to define and develop 'country parks', within which they can take bold initiatives to provide for many outdoor recreational needs. Country zones were first proposed in the *South East Strategy* of the South East Economic Planning Council (1967), and were conceived to have an essentially defensive role, protecting the rural economy, safeguarding agricultural land and resisting urbanization. On a larger scale, national parks, forest parks and, in Scotland, areas of outstanding scenic beauty have been designated, with national and international as well as local needs in mind.

The territorial extent of these many land-use controls that are used to deny, to mute or to deflect development pressures in Britain is shown in Figure 4. Many of these areas are administered by the local planning authorities. The larger areas, however, especially the National Parks and the Forest Parks, are under the administration of the Countryside Commission and the Forestry Commission, both national bodies (Central Office of Information 1972).

4.3 *New Towns*

A much more positive measure available to governments seeking to influence the pattern of intra-regional development is centered upon the notion of the New Town. It is a measure that has been exploited with singular boldness by British planning authorities. After World War II, the ideas of Ebenezer Howard and the Garden Cities Movement were wedded to a need to provide a considerable amount of housing beyond the metropolitan green belt as part of the Abercrombie plan for Greater London. Population which could not be housed in a physically constrained Greater London was to be guided through overspill policies into a series of medium-sized communities lying between 40 and 50 kilometres from the centre of the conurbation. The idea was to create communities with not only a high quality of urban environment, but also with substantial opportunities for local employment. There were already two prototypes for these New Towns, one at Letchworth (1902) and the other at Welwyn Garden City (1920), both of which had been built and financed by

Figure 4   Areas of major policy restraints upon land-use changes in Britain, 1974

private enterprise. The major innovation after 1945 was the provision of public funds
for New-Town construction under the 1946 New Towns Act, and the appointment
for each community of a Development Corporation with powers of compulsory
land purchase. The Development Corporation was appointed by the government and
was responsible for acquiring land, preparing plans and supervising the growth of the
new communities. Initially eight New Towns were designated in the South East of the
country to meet the overspill needs of London. Others were designated in Scotland
(mostly to provide for Glasgow's overspill requirements), and in North-East England
and South Wales (where their principal role was to inject a higher quality of urban
environment into those older industrial regions). At a later date, in the 1960s, still
more New Towns were designated in North-West England, the West Midlands and
once again in the South East, to assist with conurbation overspill, and also in Northern

28

Ireland. The pattern of New-Town designation in the United Kingdom is shown in Figure 5.

Figure 5 New and Expanding Towns in Britain, 1974

4.3.1 Expanded towns

As an alternative to the New-Town mechanism, the Town Development Act of 1952 permitted and helped to finance special overspill arrangements between the large conurbation authorities and any local authority elsewhere in the country. These Expanded Towns have the advantage that they permit quite small-scale movement to some places; they also avoid for the government the New-Town problem of having to designate substantial green-field areas for urban growth against the wishes of local interests; and they have the further advantage that they blend new and old urban development, thereby avoiding some of the problems of entirely new communities. This latter advantage was grasped on a larger scale in the 1960s when two quite large communities, Northampton and Peterborough, were designated for major expansion – but this time, once again, under the auspices of the 1946 New Towns Act. A list of the country's new and expanded towns is given in Table A1 (in Appendix).

29

4.3.2 *Changing concepts*   Ideas surrounding the New-Town concept and its role in public attempts to shape
more deliberately the geography of urban growth have changed significantly over the
last twenty-five years. In the first place, the preferred size of the new or overspill
communities has tended to get larger. Whilst in the 1950s the general preference was
for communities of between 40,000 and 60,000, by the late 1960s new communities
were being designated with plans for an eventual population of between 200,000 and
250,000 people. One explanation of this trend is to be found in economic factors, for
there is clear evidence that the unit costs of the infrastructure and public facilities in
the larger new communities are lower than in the smaller ones. A further explanation
is to be found in the changes of average life-styles and social preferences: the increased
range of goods, services and amenities that are required or preferred by the average
household of today in comparison with a household of the 1950s can be provided only
in the market afforded by the larger communities.

Another changing feature of the New Towns is the much wider range of employments
and activities that have come to be located in them. Obviously, this characteristic is
influenced strongly by the size and the location of the town, and it is certainly the case
that many New Towns in the development areas still tend to be built upon an
economic base of manufacturing industry. The London New Towns were also
dominated by manufacturing industry until the early 1960s. Since then, however, they
have come to attract an ever-growing variety of employment opportunities in the
fields of research and development, national services, and the office sector in general.
The result has been that, in economic terms, these New Towns have become
extraordinarily well-balanced communities and, with only a small percentage of
unskilled jobs, they now exhibit higher standards of living than the national average.

Time has also eroded earlier notions about the spatial role of New Towns.
Abercrombie espoused a notion that, in terms of employment and a wide range of local
services, the New Towns could be self-sufficient. To a large extent this is till true
today. However, increasingly there is a tendency for the New Towns to become more
closely integrated into a wider sub-regional economy and society – offering
employment to people living outside the designated areas, providing accommodation
for people working elsewhere, serving as sub-regional shopping centres, and providing
a growing list of services to a population well beyond their designated areas. In fact, it
has become necessary to interpret the whole set of overspill mechanisms, not so much
in terms of checking conurbation expansion, as they were in the past, but more in
terms of devices to guide and shape the geography of metropolitan expansion. To
achieve this end, the New and Expanded Towns must be seen as only a part of a wider
set of public initiatives. Consider the planning of South-East England today.

4.3.3 *The Strategic Plan*   Urban development and land-use changes in the South-East region are currently
for the South East   being pursued within the framework of the 1970 *Strategic Plan for the South East*
(South East Joint Planning Team 1970). Accepting the continuing decline in the
population of Greater London, the *Strategy* calls for the guidance of the greater part of
population growth in the region into five major-growth and six medium-growth areas
located in both the Outer Metropolitan Area and the Outer South East (Figure 6). In
some of these growth areas, the New-Towns mechanism is being employed to
facilitate development. In the Milton Keynes major-growth area, there is both the new
city of Milton Keynes and (beyond the region) Northampton. The Reading/
Aldershot/Basingstoke major-growth area contains both the New Town of Bracknell
and a substantial town expansion scheme at Basingstoke. The Crawley/Burgess Hill
major-growth area contains the New Town of Crawley. And the South Essex
major-growth area contains both Basildon New Town and, prospectively, a New
Town to be associated with the proposed Third London Airport at Maplin. Of the
medium-growth areas, three (Aylesbury, Hastings and Ashford) have expansion
schemes arranged under the Town Development Act. On the other hand, it is
noteworthy that the other major-growth area, South Hampshire, and three of the

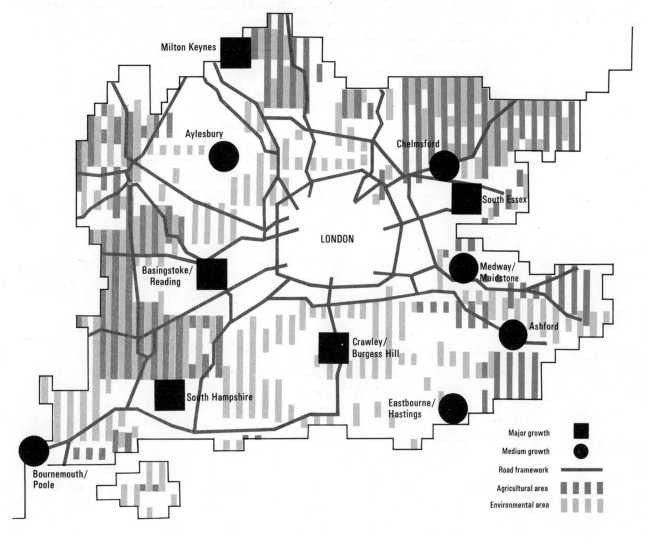

Figure 6   The Strategic Plan for the South East, 1974   Source: Department of the Environment (1973)

Legend:
- Major growth ■
- Medium growth ●
- Road framework
- Agricultural area
- Environmental area

medium-growth areas (Bournemouth/Poole, Maidstone/Medway and Chelmsford) are currently not being developed either with the New-Towns mechanism or the assistance of funds from the Town Development Act.

In explanation, the first point to be made is that the primary mechanism for handling urban growth in South-East England is the land and property market, constrained by local development plans. It should be recalled that during the post-war years the London New Towns provided accommodation for only about 13 per cent of the population leaving Greater London; the rest were accommodated by other public housing schemes (such as the Town Development Act and local council houses) and private development. There are, however, some circumstances in which it is judged that central-government initiatives are imperative in regional development; particularly is this so when a conflict arises between national and regional priorities on the one hand, and local preferences on the other. This conflict is real. Local authorities beyond a large conurbation, for example, are frequently dominated by rural or middle- and upper-income ex-urban interests, and it is frequently the case that these interests come to be reflected in local land-use plans. In order to assert broader (both geographical and social) interests, therefore, it is sometimes necessary for the New-Towns mechanism to be employed, and to override local resistance to land-use changes and major urban developments.

Another situation in which the designation of a New Town appears to be appropriate occurs when rapid urban development is planned in a locality and sub-region that has only a small population and limited financial and professional resources. By steering national resources through the hands of a Development Corporation the government can foster rapid economic development in places where it would otherwise occur only very slowly, if at all. It is certainly very difficult to envisage rapid and large-scale urban expansion in a locality with a small population and economic base, without the New-Towns machinery; the new city of Milton Keynes provides a case in point. Yet another circumstance in which the designation of a New Town appears to be particularly appropriate to intra-regional development needs occurs when major urban expansion is planned in a sub-region embracing several local authorities. Whilst the coordination of their efforts and plans through existing or new *ad hoc* channels is a feasible solution to the problems presented by such a situation, the Development Corporation does afford opportunities for a more decisive style of planning and development. There are some observers who believe that the Reading/Aldershot/ Basingstoke major-growth area should be given some form of New-Town status in order to coordinate the plans and initiatives of the four county authorities that are involved with its development.

4.4 Infrastructure investments

In a sense, government decisions in regard to New-Town designation and construction are but one facet of larger mechanism by which, through the provision of large infrastructural investments, the government has a decisive means of shaping the pattern of regional development. The provision of motorways and roads, the support of rail services, the allocation of funds for major sewage schemes and the provision of water supply are all part of the inevitable role of government; and their size, timing and location is crucial to the evolution of land uses and spatial change.

Of these several infrastructural investments, transport facilities are amongst the most important. Yet up to the middle 1960s, it is fair to argue that transport policies were rarely related to the broader objectives of regional and sub-regional planning in Britain. Transport investments were supervised by a Ministry of Transport that took little note of the policies being developed by the Ministry of Housing and Local Government, then responsible for intra-regional planning. Old roads were improved and new roads were constructed in response to criteria that were designed to reflect in a crude fashion the level and growth of demand, and that were constrained by the costs of adjusting the built environment within large urban areas to the rising level of vehicle ownership and use. The railway system was simultaneously adjusted to the shifting demands of the market, and was contracted as its use was steadily eroded by the growth of road transport. Airports, supervised by yet another Ministry, were expanded in response to traffic growth and with little regard to their sub-regional impacts. Since the middle 1960s, however, a great deal of progress has been made to bridge the previous divide between transport and regional planning. The Ministry of Transport has been placed within the Department of the Environment. Airport policy has been placed firmly within a regional-planning context. Only seaport development has remained largely uncommitted to the regional-development stage. Whilst the desirability, however, of encouraging a close relationship between regional planning and transport policies and investment has been widely accepted, the means to achieve this estimable end have proved to be somewhat elusive.

4.4.1 Some problems

The inter-relationship of inter-urban trunk road improvement and the broad strategy of regional development is readily appreciated. In consequence, it has not been difficult to ensure that substantial proposals for urban development are either related to the existing motorway or trunk road system, or are backed by a decision to invest in new road facilities to support them. On the other hand, many of the fundamental questions of intra-urban road planning remain unresolved, to leave serious questions for land-use planning in the largest conurbations. The impasse over the ringway motorway proposals for Greater London are a case in point. Having been planned by the Greater London Council in association with its 1969 Structure Plan, these roads were criticized first by the general public and later by the Layfield Enquiry (into the *Greater London Development Plan* – Department of the Environment 1973) on grounds of their cost, their associated environmental damage and their uncertain economic and spatial effects. Having been withdrawn by a new Greater London Council, by early 1974 the ringway proposals had not been replaced by any alternative schemes to ensure the efficiency of circulation within the sub-region, with the result that grave uncertainty continued to hang over the allocation of new land uses within the conurbation.

In the sphere of public transport investment and operation this uncertainty is compounded. Bus services within Greater London suffer from severe shortages of labour for maintenance and operations, and transport planning remains bewildered by the need to decide upon the type, quality and regularity of service in the absence of a long-term pricing policy and the erosion of market guidelines. Rail services have been subject to constantly changing public attitudes and policies in recent years. Underground, the capital costs of new facilities have been justified by social benefits in the cases of the new Victoria and Fleet lines – but it is not at all clear that these measures will be applied to all other proposed extensions to the system. The surface commuter rail services have been the object of fluctuating government pricing policies, with decisions to remove the central-government operating subsidies quickly being followed by a reversal of that policy. While the close relationship between transport policy and regional development has been widely appreciated, therefore, the development and implementation of a coherent and sustained transport policy have proved to be somewhat elusive in all but the most obvious of cases.

4.4.2 The Third London Airport

One such case was the proposed Third London Airport. When burgeoning air traffic and growing congestion at London Airport (Heathrow) during the middle 1960s suggested that, in addition to London Airport (Gatwick), a further major airport facility for the London region would be needed within a decade or so, the authorities proposed the expansion of an existing but small airport at Stansted in Essex. Within a short time, however, articulate local opposition to the scheme developed and changed the government's initial inclination to endorse the proposal – an inclination which was, in fact, at variance with the regional-planning strategy, which sought to retain the sector of the Outer Metropolitan Area containing Stansted as part of the metropolitan green belt. The government instead established the Roskill Commission to advise on a site for a Third London Airport, and after one of the most elaborate planning exercises of all time the Commission found itself divided and produced both a majority and a minority report. The government of the day elected to place greater weight on the latter, which sought to place greater emphasis on intuitive, environmental judgements; it ruled against the most economic inland site, and in due course designated the coastal Maplin as the chosen location.

The Roskill Commission on the Third London Airport provided the first occasion in Britain when an attempt was made publicly to balance all the many, and at times contradictory, factors which should be considered in such a locational decision. The four sites from which a final choice was made were tested in the light of regional-planning objectives. The importance of doing so is demonstrated by the evidence that the airport could in time generate, on and near to the site, up to 65,000 jobs, which in turn might be associated with an urbanization in the airport sub-region of as many as 200,000 people. Whatever the criticisms that might be levelled at the Roskill Commission's work (Adams 1971) or the final outcome of events (for subsequent traffic forecasts, lowered in response to larger aircraft and higher fuel costs, and capital shortages may occasion an indefinite postponement of the Maplin construction), there can be little doubt that the Third London Airport enquiry represented a major advance in the procedures of regional planning. For the first time, not only were most of the right questions asked, but a serious attempt was made to forecast the spatial implications of a major infrastructural investment before it was built. It remains for the methodology to be improved; and at some time, the questions asked by the Roskill Commission at the intra-regional scale must be faced at the inter-regional scale also.

| 4.5 | *Location of government employments* | Government is a major employer. A supplementary weapon in its armoury to influence intra-regional patterns of development is to locate its offices and facilities with spatial planning considerations in mind. In 1963, the civil service in Britain totalled 690,000 staff, of whom 502,200 were in the non-industrial service. Of these latter, 356,500, or 70 per cent, were located outside Greater London (defined as more than 25 kilometres from Charing Cross). This pattern had followed from a variety of influences, not least of which were the wartime dispersal of offices for strategic regions, and the 1962 Fleming Report, which recommended the dispersal of 14,000 posts from central London and of some 5,500 to the outskirts. The Hardman proposals of 1973 recommended further dispersal. Hardman proposed the movement of 31,000 jobs from central London, of which 12,100 would be to locations within the South East. The principal beneficiary of these proposals was to have been Milton Keynes, to which Hardman would have relocated some 10,900 jobs; other centres were to be Southend, Teddington, Basingstoke and Sunningdale. In the event, it is clear that the Milton Keynes total will be lower and that a somewhat more scattered pattern will emerge. |

Beyond the civil service there are undoubtedly a large number of employments within the public sector which could also be made subject to more deliberate employment-location policies. The size of the headquarters staffs of the nationalized industries, for example, which remain quite substantial in the central areas of London, might reasonably be questioned. In local government many activities have clearly to be conducted in locations that are relatively accessible to the populations they serve, yet a number of options are often available within many regions and sub-regions. The decision of the former Monmouthshire County Council to move its activities from Newport to Cwmbran, in order to strengthen and diversify the employment base of the New Town, is a case in point. Local and regional hospital administration, the regional offices of the electricity, gas and water authorities, and a variety of other public services are all to some extent footloose within a sub-regional economy. Although they have been neglected in the past, they could undoubtedly be used more deliberately in the future to encourage particular patterns of employment at this scale. The higher-education sector of the economy is possibly the most neglected in this regard. Universities, polytechnics, colleges of further education, art schools and the like are all characterized by a high degree of locational flexibility which could be used by strong and imaginative local and national authorities to serve wider ends. After all, a university or college for 4,000 students will provide jobs for approximately 400 teaching staff, who in turn will be assisted by an equal number of administrators, library staff, porters, cleaners and the like; within the local economy such a number of people would be serviced by perhaps a further 1,000 employees in schools, hospitals, local authority services and the like; and the students could well generate a further 1,000 jobs in shops, bars, public transport, the local constabulary and so forth. In sum, 4,000 students can well be associated with a related population of some 6,000. Such a number of relatively footloose people are worthy of more deliberate attention in regional planning than has been given them to date.

| 4.6 | *Floorspace controls* | To further supplement its principal tools of land-use allocation and development control, major initiatives in urban growth and the location of infrastructural investments, government policies at the intra-regional scale can also make use of floorspace controls. In Britain, for instance, by policies denying industrial development certificates or office development permits in particular parts of South-East England and the West Midlands, the government has been able to contribute substantially to its broad objectives of decentralization (Keeble 1972 pp 88ff). The development of the New Towns as foci of accelerated growth has undoubtedly been assisted by the fact that the relevant government departments have always looked much more favourably on applications for permission to increase industrial and office floorspace there than on locations elsewhere in the Outer Metropolitan Area. |

The present administration of office development controls is in fact quite explicit in its two principal objectives. One is to encourage the dispersal from London of those activities which could equally effectively be carried out elsewhere; this can involve either inter-regional or intra-regional movement. The second is to encourage the growth of office employment in the 'growth areas' of the South East, and at the same time to safeguard from development those parts of the region outside the growth areas, unless further office development is essential for already-established local populations and is in scale with the long-term development proposals for the areas.

One of the problems of floorspace controls is that they are inclined to distort the operations of the market and pose problems every bit as difficult as those they were designed to solve. In the case of offices, for example, there is little doubt that the limited supply of development permits in central London has caused demand to outstrip available office space, create a situation of scarcity and so inflate the cost of office activities. Even allowing for the inflation in the economy as a whole, it is noteworthy that central-London rents which stood at about £2.00–2.50 per square foot only a few years ago are now standing in the range £10.00–15.00 per square foot – four times those of New York!

In the *Greater London Development Plan* it was proposed that the control of office floorspace should be taken out of the hands of the Department of the Environment and be handled exclusively by the Greater London Council, with a view to allocating particular levels of office development to each borough. (The same proposal was also made for industrial manufacturing floorspace.) The thesis behind the proposals was that the Council would be able, through such controls, to redress any imbalance of employment opportunities throughout the Greater London area. However, the proposal was resisted by the government, partly because it was felt that the controls were better handled at a higher level, and partly because it was clear that office activities would not readily respond to a planned distribution between boroughs on the basis of an administrator's sense of equity. Of the 1,400 or so firms wishing to move within the Greater London area between 1963 and 1972, nearly 1,000 stated a preference for a move towards the south and west – a preference which is undoubtedly shaped by the geography of labour supply for office activities in the sub-region, by the quality of rail and air communications in the south-west quadrant, and by the preferences of senior management, many of whose homes lie in or beyond that zone.

4.7 Persuasion British office location policies draw attention to yet a further measure that can be employed by a government that seeks to shape the pattern of regional growth. This is the effectiveness of persuasion, and especially advertising. In response to the highly localized pattern of office activities in central London, and certain problems that were associated with it, the government established in 1963 the Location of Offices Bureau. Its remit was simple: 'to encourage the decentralisation of office employment from congested central London to suitable centres elsewhere'. In the first decade of its existence, the Bureau had nothing more than market forces (blunted by locational inertia) and persuasion to achieve its objectives. In consequence nearly half of its funds each year have been spent on advertising and publicity of various sorts – all to demonstrate the advantages to office management of considering alternative locations for their business activities, and (in more recent years) to make the logic of the market more transparent. Because of the variety of forces that play upon the location decisions of office managements, it is impossible to provide a scientific answer to questions which seek to explore the effectiveness of advertising and publicity. There can be little doubt, however, that over time the Bureau has made the office industry much more self-conscious about its locational behaviour, and, backing its publicity with a substantial body of relevant and perceptive research, has been a notable influence upon the geography of office employment in the country.

Advertising and publicity by central government can be, and is, supplemented by similar activities at the sub-regional scale. Particularly for the purpose of attracting a new or an alternative economic base, the Development Corporations of New Towns and local authorities have both spent an increasing amount of money on advertising. By spelling out the areas' general attractions to industrial development, and by making more widely known the facilities that they already have available for an incoming manufacturer or office employer, such publicity has a valid role to play. Given the limited amount of mobile industry and offices that are available in any one year, it can be argued that much of this publicity is self-cancelling, and that the public funds that are usually employed could be put to better use. Nevertheless, evidence does exist that publicity and advertising can really raise the level of interest in, and the rate of movement to, particular places. To the extent that, at any one time, the urgency of the need for further industries, offices and employments varies from place to place, the timing of advertising campaigns is well able to reflect needs and to a greater or lesser degree to satisfy them.

5   *Conclusion*   The ability of governments to shape the pattern of regional development at all scales provides a fascinating field of geographical study. The variety of measures that can be adopted in response to different economic, political, social and environmental objectives is all too apparent. However, there remain many questions and uncertainties concerning the effectiveness of particular measures in particular circumstances, and the true costs that need to be associated with the benefits achieved. The rising costs and the unselective nature of the inducements currently used in British inter-regional policy are a cause for concern, as has already been noted; similarly, the expense of present practices in land-use allocation and development control at the intra-regional scale, including the scarcities that are so frequently generated, demands much more investigation. Whilst these costs have to date been accepted by governments and the general public alike, it is increasingly apparent that, as the costs continue to grow, the debate surrounding their size, their timing and the geography of their application will become increasingly vigorous. It is a debate that geographical analysis and intuition can usefully inform.

Appendix (see p 29)

Table A1 Progress in the New and Expanded towns in the United Kingdom, 1937 (pp 38–42)

Table A1 (a)   New Towns

Table A1 (b)   Expanded towns, summary

Table A1 (c)   Expanded towns, details

Table A1 (d)   Overspill agreements in Scotland

Source: *Town and Country Planning*, January 1974.

(a) New Towns, December 1973

	Date of designation	Designated area in acres and (in brackets) hectares		Population		
				Original	Proposed	31 Dec. 1973
LONDON RING						
Basildon	4 Jan. 1949	7,818	(3,165)	25,000	103,600 134,000	84,000
Bracknell	17 June 1949	3,303	(1,336)	5,140	50–60,000 50–60,000	40,000
Crawley	9 Jan. 1947	5,920	(2,396)	9,100	— 85,000	71,000
Harlow	25 Mar. 1947	6,395	(2,588)	4,500	undecided	81,000
Hatfield	20 May 1948	2,340	(947)	8,500	— 29,000	26,000
Hemel Hempstead	4 Feb. 1947	5,910	(2,392)	21,000	65,000 80,000	73,000
Stevenage	11 Nov. 1946	6,256	(2,532)	6,700	80,000 100–105,000	74,000
Welwyn Garden City	20 May 1948	4,317	(1,747)	18,500	— 50,000	41,400
Total: London Ring	—	42,259	(17,103)	98,440	—	490,400
OTHERS IN ENGLAND						
Aycliffe	19 Apr. 1947	2,508	(1,003)	60	40,000 45,000	24,300
Central Lancs.	26 Mar. 1970	35,225	(14,250)	235,638	420,000 420,000	240,500
Corby	1 Apr. 1950	4,296	(1,790)	15,700	undecided 83,000	51,000
Milton Keynes	23 Jan. 1967	22,000	(8,900)	40,000	200,000 250,000	60,000
Northampton	14 Feb. 1968	19,966	(8,080)	131,120	230,000 260,000	141,000
Peterborough	1 Aug. 1967	15,952	(6,461)	81,000	182,000 n.a.	96,400
Peterlee	10 Mar. 1948	2,799	(1,133)	200	28,000 30,000	26,300
Redditch	10 Apr. 1964	7,180	(2,906)	32,000	70,000 90,000	45,760
Runcorn	10 Apr. 1964	7,234	(2,927)	30,000	70–75,000 100,000	43,680
Skelmersdale	9 Oct. 1961	4,124	(1,668)	10,000	73,300 80,000	38,500
Telford	12 Dec. 1968	19,300	(7,790)	73,000	225,000 250,000	91,000
Warrington	26 Apr. 1968	18,612	(7,535)	122,300	201,500 225,000	132,000
Washington	26 July 1964	5,610	(2,271)	20,000	65,000 80,000	35,000
Total: Others in England	—	164,806	(66,714)	791,018	—	1,025,440
WALES						
Cwmbran	4 Nov. 1949	3,160	(1,275)	12,000	55,000 55,000	43,000
Mid-Wales (Newtown)	18 Dec. 1967	1,497	(606)	5,500	11,000 13,000	6,600
Total: Wales	—	4,657	(1,881)	17,500	—	49,600
Total: England & Wales	—	211,722	(85,698)	906,958	—	1,565,440
SCOTLAND						
Cumbernauld	9 Dec. 1955	7,788	(3,152)	3,000	70,000 100,000	36,000
East Kilbride	6 May 1947	10,250	(4,148)	2,400	82,500 90–100,000	69,100
Glenrothes	30 June 1948	5,765	(2,333)	1,100	55,000 70,000	32,000
Irvine	9 Nov. 1966	12,440	(5,022)	34,600	100,000 120,000	48,400
Livingston	17 Apr. 1962	6,692	(2,708)	2,000	70,000 100,000	20,000
Stonehouse	24 July 1973	6,765	(2,738)	7,250	45,000 70,000	7,350
Total: Scotland	—	49,700	(20,101)	50,350	—	212,850
Total: Great Britain	—	261,422	(105,799)	957,308	—	1,778,290
NORTHERN IRELAND						
Antrim	7 July 1966	119,540	(48,653)	32,600	70,000 74,000	41,000
Ballymena	29 June 1967	161,306	(65,652)	48,000	90,000 96,000	56,000
Craigavon	July 1965	67,200	(26,880)	60,800	127,000 180,000	74,000
Londonderry	5 Feb. 1969	85,522	(34,610)	82,000	94,000 100,000	n.a.

Manufacturing Industry						Offices					
Before designation			Completed from designation to 31 Dec. 1973 (est.)			Offices existing before designation (est.)[1]			Offices completed from designation to 31 Dec. 1973		
No. of occupiers	No. of employees	Size (sq. ft.)	No. of occupiers	No. of employees	Size (sq. ft.)	No. of offices	No. of employees	Size (sq. ft.)	No. of offices	No. of employees	Size (sq. ft.)
20	438	144,714	180	21,076	5,977,975	—	—	—	50	n.k.	366,930
7	179	48,250	67	9,721	2,540,284	n.k.	n.k.	n.k.	77	6,250	861,675
23	1,529	222,000	92	20,490	4,829,699	—	—	—	63	2,600	421,370
6	333	n.k.	294§	18,918	6,313,221	—	—	—	101	2,687	627,899
8	900	10,000	20+8 extns	1,568	438,650	16	n.k.	n.k.	17	n.k.	32,800
36	6,200	n.k.	76	14,000	4,009,482	n.k.	n.k.	n.k.	53	3,200	675,420
5	2,200	371,000	37	16,100	3,416,000	n.k.	n.k.	n.k.	66	2,400	387,000
69	10,000	1,994,594	23+18 extns	3,981	1,473,900	18	500	18,000	49	750	189,184
174	21,779	—	789+26 extns	105,854	28,999,211	—	—	—	476	—	3,562,278
97	8,994	3,486,297	1	264	60,826	—	—	—	14	n.k.	31,300
1,480	63,000	22,800,000	—	—	—	950	33,000	3,000,000	n.a.	n.a.	n.a.
3	n.k.	n.k.	41	5,092	1,323,573	n.k.	n.k.	n.k.	39	1,595	213,348
86	12,000	n.k.	80	2,113	1,007,200	n.k.	n.k.	180,000	9	n.a.	226,350
419	29,200	7,526,000	147	9,400	1,866,000	491	5,400	965,004	30	5,700	941,000
n.k.	45,500	6,290,000	n.k.	10,200	1,059,000	n.k.	6,000	756,250	n.k.	380	57,000
—	—	—	48	4,790	1,374,044	—	—	—	26	320	67,916
108	12,600	3,413,750	185	5,177	2,063,630	180	n.k.	163,727	29	n.k.	233,245
30	8,000	n.k.	77	2,273	1,171,670	41	n.k.	n.k.	22	1,423	331,218
12	981	328,078	84	9,500	3,599,407	8	21	2,210	28	500	72,718
100	16,000	5,300,000	170	4,500	2,012,000	124	1,540	320,000	16	460	75,000
n.k.	32,800	5,401,440	8	40	112,000	n.k.	13,100	533,500	—	—	—
10	3,614	759,375	135	6,308	2,208,986	n.k.	n.k.	n.k.	22	852	176,943
—	232,689+	—	976+	59,657	17,858,336	—	—	—	—	—	2,426,038+
20	6,800	1,500,000	95	4,768	959,453	n.k.	n.k.	n.k.	22	920	136,810
7	900	350,000	27	650	175,230	28	230	80,000	2	30	10,000
27	7,700	1,850,000	122	5,418	1,134,683	—	—	—	24	950	146,810
—	262,168+	—	1,887+26 extns	170,929	47,992,230	—	—	—	—	—	6,135,126+
3	171	151,000	143	6,056	2,725,779	1	5	3,200	58	1,137	222,679
3	314	173,200	275	17,290	5,727,615	9	50	9,470	81	2,750	425,030
4	1,884	750,000	115	8,203	2,290,591	—	—	—	53	800	135,601
58	6,000	2,479,000	74	6,600	1,716,119	97	1,600	100,000	n.k.	500	30,782
3	70	89,500	55	4,250	2,014,365	—	—	—	21	620	67,074
6	790	90,750	—	—	—	7	30	6,570	—	—	—
77	9,229	3,733,450	662	42,399	14,474,469	114	1,685	119,240	213+	5,807	881,166
—	271,397+	—	2,549+26 extns	213,328	62,466,699	—	—	—	—	—	7,016,292+
5	1,700	564,550	55	3,350	1,074,275	36	200	30,500	2	4	1,500
107	5,920	2,275,200	15	2,710	1,056,465	63	300	40,000	55	436	68,000
n.k.	13,227	n.k.	78	7,500	2,800,000	n.k.	n.k.	n.k.	n.k.	n.k.	n.k.
n.k.	n.k.	n.k.	n.a.	n.a.	n.a.	n.k.	n.k.	n.k.	n.a.	n.a.	n.a.

(b) Town Development Act progress summarized to 30 June 1973

Exporting area	Number of schemes agreed	Dwellings for letting			Factories (area in thousand sq. ft.)	
		To be built	Completed	Under construction	Completed	Under construction
Greater London	32	93,049	50,013	2,829	28,963.9	3,155.2
Birmingham	15	21,122	10,185	296	4,773.3	819.9
Bristol	4*	2,278	2,278	—	—	—
Liverpool	4	18,526	5,929	30	2,999.4	113.0
Manchester	4	8,514	1,373	5	762.1	56.1
Newcastle upon Tyne	2	10,517	2,252	71	2,711.9	954.4
Salford	1*	4,518	4,518	—	—	—
Walsall	2*	444	444	—	—	—
Wolverhampton	4	4,527	4,470	57	67.5	—
All schemes	68	163,495	81,462	3,288	40,278.1	5,098.6

The table includes the following schemes which were completed in the years shown (in brackets number of dwellings)   *=scheme completed

GREATER LONDON	Completed in
Canvey Island UD (414)	1962
Frimley and Camberley UD (1,177)	1964
Luton CB (1,000)	1965
Peterborough B (132) (scheme taken over by development corporation)	1968

BIRMINGHAM

Banbury B (235)	1966
Uttoxeter UD (200)	1965
Tutbury RD (60)	1971
Leek UD (100)	1971

(The last two schemes have been terminated: at Tutbury 49 dwellings were built, none at Leek)

BRISTOL	Completed in
Keynsham UD (642)	1960
Sudbury RD (136)	1966
Thornbury RD (500)	1966
Warmley RD (1,000)	1961

SALFORD

Worsley UD (4,518)	1966

WALSALL	Completed in
Aldridge UD (215)	1960
Brownhills UD (229)	1958

WOLVERHAMPTON

Selsdon RD (1,546)	1964
Tettenhall UD (131)	1966
Wednesfield UD (2,450)	1966

(c) Town Development Act progress (England and Wales) to 30 June 1973

Dispersing area	Expanding towns	Dwellings for letting			Factories Completed		Factories Under construction
		To be built	Completed	Under construc-tion	No. of firms	Area (thousand sq. ft)	Area (thousand sq. ft)
Greater London	Andover B	6,000	2,290	347	58	1,207.5	120.8
	Ashford UD	4,250	1,954	206	31	879.2	75.1
	Aylesbury B	3,700	2,317	90	45	946.2	12.2
	Banbury B	2,000	1,311	100	27	2,221.7	29.0
	Basingstoke B	9,250	5,691	777	89	3,026.4	213.9
	Bletchley UD	5,000	4,551	429	73	1,996.8	264.4
	Bodmin B	500	134	50	28	172.1	32.5
	Braintree and Bocking UD	1,200	331	—	14	136.0	60.0
	Burnley CB	700	86	—	—	—	—
	Bury St Edmunds B	3,000	1,222	23	36	466.1	27.0
	Gainsborough UD	1,000	115	—	20	297.2	16.3
	Grantham B	500	20	—	—	—	—
	Hastings CB	2,850	—	—	—	—	—
	Haverhill UD	4,500	2,524	—	54	1,260.1	120.7
	Huntingdon and Godmanchester B	2,450	2,006	74	40	753.5	42.0
	Kings Lynn B	3,500	1,324	114	48	1,355.8	189.3
	Letchworth UD	1,500	1,433	78	15	117.0	18.0
	Luton RD	3,896	1,870	114	—	—	—
	Melford RD	750	724	—	20	217.8	71.0
	Mildenhall RD	2,000	831	73	73	523.1	78.7
	Plymouth CB	3,000	130	50	2	424.4	—
	St Neots UD	2,000	1,019	250	30	782.1	73.1
	Sandy UD	700	186	—	14	118.2	10.1
	Sudbury B	1,500	386	30	6	27.4	3.6
	Swindon B	8,580	8,016	24	91	7,108.4	1,363.3
	Thetford B	3,000	2,590	—	77	1,827.8	143.4
	Wellingborough UD	10,000	2,204	—	41	1,615.0	66.0
	Witham UD	3,000	2,025	—	17	1,484.1	124.8
	Current schemes	90,326	47,290	2,829	949	28,963.9	3,155.2
	Completed schemes	2,723	2,723	—	—	—	—
	Total for Greater London	93,049	50,013	2,829	949	28,963.9	3,155.2
Birmingham	Aldridge-Brownhills UD	2,400	938	—	30	293.4	23.2
	Cannock UD	500	474	26	—	—	—
	Daventry B	5,275	1,711	93	41	2,712.2	402.6
	Droitwich B	2,000	1,375	60	33	511.0	111.6
	Lichfield B	1,200	973	—	—	—	—
	Lichfield RD	500	66	—	—	—	—
	Rugeley UD	300	130	—	10	173.7	—
	Stafford B	750	389	32	—	—	—
	Stafford RD	300	—	—	—	—	—
	Tamworth B	6,500	2,843	85	44	730.0	282.5
	Current schemes	19,725	8,899	296	158	4,420.3	819.9
	Completed schemes	1,397	1,286	—	12	353.0	—
	Total for Birmingham	21,122	10,185	296	170	4,773.3	819.9
Wolverhampton	Cannock RD	400	343	57	—	—	—
	Completed schemes	4,127	4,127	—	11	67.5	—
	Total for Wolverhampton	4,527	4,470	57	11	67.5	—
Liverpool	Burnley CB	2,200	66	—	—	—	—
	Ellesmere Port B	5,500	2,383	30	—	—	—
	Widnes B	4,160	853	—	18	477.8	—
	Winsford UD	6,666	2,627	—	39	2,521.6	113.0
	Total for Liverpool	18,526	5,929	30	57	2,999.4	113.0
Manchester	Burnley CB	2,700	14	—	—	—	—
	Crewe B	4,000	45	5	—	—	—
	Macclesfield B	1,250	750	—	29	762.1	56.1
	Current schemes	7,950	809	5	29	762.1	56.1
	Winsford UD	564	564	—	—	—	—
	Total for Manchester	8,514	1,373	5	29	762.1	56.1
Newcastle upon Tyne	Seaton Valley UD (Cramlington)	6,500	892	—	23	1,898.1	946.4
	Longbenton UD (Killingworth)	4,017	1,360	71	36	813.8	8.0
	Total for Newcastle upon Tyne	10,517	2,252	71	59	2,711.9	954.4

(d) Scotland: Overspill agreements to 31 March 1973

Receiving area	Date of agreement	Houses to be built by local authority	Houses to be built by SSHA	Total houses to be built under agreements	Total houses completed at 31 March 1973
Alloa	16 Dec. 1959	50	25	75	68
Alva	6 Nov. 1963	50	—	50	2
Arbroath	26 Feb. 1959	300	98	398	193
Barrhead	16 May 1963	82	128	210	210
Bathgate	11 June 1963	120	157	277	193
Bonnyrigg and Lasswade	23 Feb. 1961	50	50	100	70
Denny and Dunipace	12 Jan. 1960	250	250	500	396
Dumbarton	19 Feb. 1963	200	72	272	72
Dumfries	13 Mar. 1962	100	—	100	12
Dunbar	29 Sept. 1961	150	46	196	124
Dunbarton County	6 Feb. 1964	200	149	349	173
Forfar	21 Dec. 1959	150	—	150	—
Fort William	26 Apr. 1962	100	100	200	100
Galashiels	1 June 1960	50	50	100	100
Galston	13 June 1961	100	—	100	3
Girvan	6 Mar. 1959	350	350	700	50
Grangemouth	8 Sept. 1958	350	347	697	681
Haddington	8 Sept. 1958	125	125	250	250
Hamilton	2 Dec. 1958	200	188	388	360
Hawick	4 Feb. 1963	50	68	118	132
Invergordon	13 Mar. 1961	50	—	50	1
Inverkeithing	12 Oct. 1962	200	200	400	254
Inverness County	25 Feb. 1963	100	—	100	108
Irvine	18 Feb. 1959	700	539	1,239	744
Jedburgh	21 Feb. 1962	250	—	250	—
Johnstone (3 agreements)	14 June 1965 latest	827	1,093	1,920	1,671
Kelso	8 Mar. 1963	50	25	75	25
Kilsyth	22 Sept. 1967	50	52	102	102
Kirkintilloch (2 agreements)	16 Feb. 1961	450	566	1,016	891
Maybole	11 Jan. 1967	180	180	360	—
Midlothian	8 Mar. 1961	500	250	750	157
Newmilns and Greenholm	25 Nov. 1963	100	—	100	12
Peebles	4 July 1961	100	32	132	52
Peebles County	26 Apr. 1965	10	10	20	20
Renfrew County (3 agreements)	17 Aug. 1967	702	4,023	4,725	2,416
Selkirk	17 Oct. 1962	50	15	65	22
Stevenston	15 Sept. 1961	25	25	50	47
Stewarton	17 June 1960	250	150	400	240
Sutherland County	19 Dec. 1960	50	—	50	—
West Lothian (Blackburn)	14 Dec. 1960	300	—	300	300
Whitburn	4 Apr. 1960	250	321	571	571
Wick	21 Aug. 1961	300	—	300	—
Sub-total		8,521	9,684	18,205	10,822
New towns					
Cumbernauld (4 agreements)	10 July 1968 latest	6,000	—	6,000	7,450
East Kilbride (5 agreements)	23 Nov. 1970 latest	6,500	—	6,500	10,993
Glenrothes	13 Nov. 1958	1,800	—	1,800	815
Irvine	—	—	—	—	255
Livingston	6 Feb. 1964	1,000	—	1,000	1,540
Sub-total		15,300	—	15,300	21,053
Grand total		23,821	9,684	33,505	31,875

SAQ 1   To the extent that spatial rather than structural factors are responsible for a regional problem, what policy measures have been devised to ameliorate the situation?

SAQ 2   Outline the principal policy adopted by the British government to support the shipbuilding industry, a staple industry located in the older industrial areas.

SAQ 3   List some of the major incentives offered to manufacturing industry to locate or expand in the Assisted Areas.

SAQ 4   In which ways has the British government encouraged the growth of employment opportunities in the service industry in the less prosperous regions?

SAQ 5   'Migration policy is both tentative and weakly developed'. Illustrate this generalization from recent British experience.

SAQ 6   What criteria, besides a high level of unemployment, might be used to delimit an area eligible for development assistance from public funds?

SAQ 7   List some of the difficulties in estimating the full costs of regional development programmes.

SAQ 8   For what reasons are green belts designated?

SAQ 9   In what ways has the notion of a New Town changed in recent decades?

SAQ 10   What floorspace controls have been used by central government in Britain to influence the geography of employments, both intra- and inter-regionally?

Answers to self-assessment Questions

SAQ 1   By improving the provision of transport facilities and services, and by pricing those services in such a way as to alter the meaning and the costs of distance, governments can radically alter the economic prospects and the rate of growth of particular areas and regions.

SAQ 2   In the case of the *shipbuilding* industry, the principal device was the creation of the Shipbuilding Industry Board in 1967; with access to over £200 million, its objective was to speed up the modernization of the yards on the precondition that the component firms would merge into larger and more viable units.

SAQ 3   Regional development grants in machinery, plant and buildings; selective assistance loans or interest-relief grants; government factories for rent or for sale; tax allowances on machinery, plant and buildings; a regional employment premium; training assistance with new workers, and grants to transfer key workers; preference for contracts placed by government departments and nationalized industries.

SAQ 4   During the 1960s the major effort was in the location of the civil service, and a policy of transferring work from London was pursued from 1962 onwards. This was complemented in 1973 by the first incentives to private office employers to transfer their activities to the Assisted Areas; removal grants and rent subsidies were the principal inducements.

43

SAQ 5 Grants are available to workers in industrial training schemes that involve a change of home; and grants are available to workers in Development Areas who are prepared to move their home in order to secure employment. However, in 1972 less than £3 million was spent on encouraging labour mobility, compared with the approximately £1,000 million that was spent on job creation in the Assisted Areas.

SAQ 6 A high level of out-migration; a low activity rate; low levels of personal income; a large proportion of employment in declining industries; evidence of underemployment (in agricultural areas especially).

SAQ 7 It is not easy to quantify (regional) differential expenditures on infrastructure, and the full costs of assistance to declining staple trades. Moreover, all data are 'net of clawback'; that is, they do not take into account the additional government income (both tax and insurance contributions) that follow from the increased output and employment of regional policies; estimates of these figures, and the reduction in unemployment benefits, are open to debate. There are also substantial costs of regional policies that are not carried by the government.

SAQ 8 The reasons have varied through time. The most common purpose of green belts today is to restrain physically the pressures towards urban and suburban sprawl. In addition, green belts can be used to prevent the merging of nearby towns and cities, and also to preserve the special character of historic and unique urban environments.

SAQ 9 Three changes are particularly important. First, the preferred size of the New Towns has tended to get larger. Second, they are now associated with a much wider range of employment opportunities. Third, their spatial role has changed such that they are now seen as a means of shaping the geography of metropolitan expansion.

SAQ 10 Large manufacturing enterprises have been influenced by the use of industrial development certificates, issued by the Department of Industry. Large office developments have been subject to the office development permit controls, administered by the Department of the Environment.

References ADAMS, J. G. U. (1971) 'London's Third Airport', *The Geographical Journal*, Vol. 137, 1971, pp. 468–504.

CAMERON, G. and CLARK, D. B. (1966) *Industrial Movement and the Regional Problem*, Oliver and Boyd, Glasgow.

CENTRAL OFFICE OF INFORMATION (1972) *Town and Country Planning in Britain*, HMSO, London.

CENTRAL OFFICE OF INFORMATION (1972) *The New Towns of Britain*, HMSO, London.

CENTRAL OFFICE OF INFORMATION (1968) *Regional Development in Britain*, HMSO, London.

DEPARTMENT OF THE ENVIRONMENT (1973) *Report of the Panel of Enquiry, Greater London Development Plan* (Chairman: F. H. B. Layfield), 2 Vols., HMSO, London.

DEPARTMENT OF THE ENVIRONMENT (1973) *Strategic Planning in the South East: a First Report of the Monitoring Group*, HMSO, London.

DEPARTMENT OF TRADE AND INDUSTRY (1974) *Incentives for Industry in the Areas for Expansion*, HMSO, London.

GREATER LONDON COUNCIL (1969) *Greater London Development Plan: Report of Studies*, GLC, London.

HARDMAN, H. (1973) *A Review of the Possibility of Dispersing More Government Work from London*, HMSO, London.

HOUSE OF COMMONS EXPENDITURE COMMITTEE (1974) *Regional Development Incentives: Report*, HMSO, London.

KEEBLE, D. E. (1972) 'The South East and East Anglia', in Manners *et al* (1972) pp. 72–152.

LUTTRELL, W. F. (1962) *Factory Location and Industrial Movement*, N.I.E.S.R., London.

MANNERS, G. (1966) *The Severn Bridge and the Future*, TWW, Cardiff.

MANNERS, G. (1968) 'Misplacing the Smelters', *New Society*, 16 May 1968, pp. 712–13.

MANNERS, G. (1972a) 'National Perspectives', in Manners *et al* (1972) pp. 1–69.

MANNERS, G. (1972b) 'On the Mezzanine Floor: Some Reflections on Contemporary Office Location Policy', *Town and Country Planning*, April 1972, pp. 210–15.

MANNERS, G., KEEBLE, D., RODGERS, B. and WARREN, K. (1972) *Regional Development in Britain*, John Wiley, London.

MCCRONE, G. (1969) *Regional Policy in Britain*, Allen and Unwin, London (Set book).

MINISTER OF POWER (1967) *Fuel Policy* (Cmnd. 3438), HMSO, London.

MOORE, B. and RHODES, J. (1973) 'Evaluating the Effects of British Regional Economic Policy', *Economic Journal*, March 1973, pp. 87–110.

REPORT OF A COMMITTEE (1961) *Inquiry into the Scottish Economy* (Chairman: J. N. Toothill), Scottish Council, Edinburgh.

RODGERS, B. (1972) The North West and North Wales, in Manners *et al* (1972) pp. 267–326.

SALT, J. (1973) 'Workers to the Work', *Area*, Vol. 8, No. 4, pp 262–66.

SECRETARY OF STATE FOR ECONOMIC AFFAIRS (1969) *The Intermediate Areas* (Hunt Committee Report), HMSO, London.

SECRETARY OF STATE FOR INDUSTRY, TRADE AND REGIONAL DEVELOPMENT (1963) *The North East*, HMSO, London.

SECRETARY OF STATE FOR SCOTLAND (1963) *Central Scotland*, HMSO, Edinburgh.

SOUTH EAST ECONOMIC PLANNING COUNCIL (1967) *A Strategy for the South East*, HMSO, London.

SOUTH EAST JOINT PLANNING TEAM (1970) *Strategic Plan for the South East*, HMSO, London.

THOMAS, D. (1970) *London's Green Belt*, Faber & Faber, London.

WARREN, K. (1969a) 'Recent Changes in the Geographical Location of the British Steel Industry', *Geographical Journal*, 135, pp. 343–64.

WARREN, K. (1969b) 'Coastal Steelworks – A Case for Argument', *Three Banks Review*, 82, pp. 25–38.

WARREN, K. (1972) 'The North East and Scotland', in Manners *et al* (1972) pp. 361–423.

Acknowledgements   Grateful acknowledgement is made to the following sources for material used in this unit:

Figures

Figures 3 and 6: the Controller, HMSO for *Strategic Plan for the South East.*

Tables

Table 3: the Controller, HMSO for *Incentives for Industry*, 1973; *Table 5:* HMSO for *Public Expenditure, 1976-7 Cmnd. 5178*; *Tables A1 a-d:* the Editor, Town and Country Planning for pp 40-1, 47, 48-9 and 50 of *Town and Country Planning*, January 1974.

Block and Unit Titles

Block 1   **Regional Imbalance.**

Unit 1   An introductory framework.

Unit 2   Measures of regional imbalance – the case of the United Kingdom.

Block 2   **The Macro Approach – the analysis of regional change.**

Unit 3   The movement of goods between regions.

Unit 4   Export base theory and the growth and decline of regions.

Unit 5   Changing the region's role.

Unit 6   Regional growth and the movement of labour and capital.

Block 3   **The Micro Approach – economic and social surfaces.**

Unit 7   Economic and social surfaces.

Unit 8   The movement of firms.

Unit 9   Human migration.

Unit 10   The consequences of labour migration.

Unit 11   Economic complexes.

Block 4   **Government Intervention.**

Unit 12   Reasons for government intervention.

Unit 13   Methods of government intervention.

Unit 14   Economic planning in a developing country: Nigeria.

Unit 15   Economic planning in a mixed economy: United Kingdom.

Unit 16   Economic planning in a socialist country: Poland.